IN PERSON

IN PERSON

*Profiles of Researchers
in Africa, Asia,
and the Americas*

INTERNATIONAL DEVELOPMENT RESEARCH CENTRE
Ottawa • Cairo • Dakar • Johannesburg • Montevideo
Nairobi • New Delhi • Singapore

Published by the International Development Research Centre
PO Box 8500, Ottawa, ON, Canada K1G 3H9

© International Development Research Centre 1995

IDRC, Ottawa, ON CA

In person : profiles of researchers in Africa, Asia, and the Americas.
Ottawa, ON, IDRC, 1995. vii + 183 p. : ill.

/Bibliographies/, /scientists/, /research workers/, /scientific discoveries/,
/Africa/, /Asia/, /Americas/.

UDC: 929:500   ISBN 0-88936-738-8

A microfiche edition is available.

All rights reserved. No part of this publication may be reproduced, stored
in a retrieval system, or transmitted, in any form or by any means, electronic, mechanical, photocopying, or otherwise, without the prior per-
mission of the International Development Research Centre.

IDRC BOOKS endeavours to produce environmentally friendly publications. All paper used is recycled as well as recyclable. All inks and coating
are vegetable-based products.

CONTENTS

PREFACE 1

Africa

EUSÈBE ALIHONOU (*BENIN*) 4
A passionate servant of community health research, Eusèbe Alihonou is helping train tomorrow's physicians and medical researchers.

PIERRE SANÉ (*SENEGAL*) 14
As head of Amnesty International, Pierre Sané puts ideas into action in his quest to combat oppression and underdevelopment in every corner of the world.

LALA STEYN (*SOUTH AFRICA*) 24
Social researcher and community activist, Lala Steyn crosses cultural boundaries to do her part in building a new and democratic South Africa.

Asia

GELIA CASTILLO (*PHILIPPINES*) 36
A pioneer in rural sociology, Gelia Castillo has helped shape thinking in international development circles around the world.

HARI GUNASINGHAM (*SRI LANKA*) 46
An intellectual free spirit, chemist Hari Gunasingham uses innovative software to optimize efficiency in such industries as tea, food processing, and palm oil production.

JAI KRISHNA NIGAM (*INDIA*) 56
Although he began in textiles research, Jai Krishna Nigam branched out to become a tireless advocate for closer links between research and industry.

WASEY OMAR (PAKISTAN). 66
The pinnacle of Omar's distinguished career as a mechanical engineer has been the invention of a low-cost dobby that could revolutionize the textile industry in Asia.

GURSARAN TALWAR (INDIA) 74
As a biochemist, Gursaran Talwar's most remarkable achievement is no doubt the development of a safe, reliable, and reversible vaccine to prevent pregnancy in women.

VO-TONG XUAN (VIET NAM). 82
Agronomist Vo-Tong Xuan's devotion to rebuilding agriculture in Viet Nam is a major reason behind its transformation to one of the world's top three rice exporters.

ZHU ZHAOHUA (CHINA). 92
The son of a forest ranger, world-renowned forestry ecologist Zhu Zhaohua has had a positive impact on both China's ecology and its agricultural output.

PLATE — PORTRAITS OF DEVELOPMENT RESEARCH. . . 102

Latin America and the Caribbean

PILAR CERECEDA (CHILE) 114
In the extraordinary "fog-catcher" technology, geographer Pilar Cereceda sees hope for supplies of fresh water in arid regions throughout the world.

JOYCE ROBINSON (JAMAICA) 126
The first Jamaican to head her country's library service, Joyce Robinson continues to make vital contributions in teaching and information.

PALMIRA VENTOSILLA (*PERU*) 138
    Microbiologist Palmira Ventosilla and her research team use coconuts as a low-cost tool in a unique and successful malaria-control program.

Canada

GUY COLLIN (*QUEBEC*) 144
    Chemical engineer Guy Collin's expertise in the extraction and analysis of essential oils from local crops takes him from Quebec to Bolivia, Brazil, Morocco, and Rwanda.

CHARLES SCHAFER AND
JOHN NORTON SMITH (*NOVA SCOTIA*) 152
    Marine scientists Schafer and Smith draw great satisfaction from their efforts to train Chinese colleagues in the design and construction of environmentally safe harbours.

HANS SCHREIER (*BRITISH COLUMBIA*) 162
    Mountain-soil specialist Hans Schreier is a key partner in a Nepalese–Canadian research team seeking sustainable farming solutions for the Himalayas.

PATRICIA STAMP (*ONTARIO*) 172
    A native of South Africa, gender and development specialist Patricia Stamp has helped illuminate many development issues facing Africa and African women.

PREFACE

Approaching a new millenium, our world is becoming more and more reliant on knowledge. The role of research, and its ability to formulate new knowledge, will be critical to the process of solving the serious challenges that face humanity. Nowhere, perhaps, is research more crucial than in the less prosperous regions of the world — the so-called Third World — where poverty, lack of nutrition, poor health, and inequality cripple the lives of millions and the hopes of future generations.

Research in the Third World, whether it is in the realm of agriculture, health, social policy, or technology, holds the key to finding appropriate solutions to problems, rather than "transplanted" solutions made in the West, which have neither local relevance nor a record of success. The past 35 years has taught us that sustainable development can only emerge from the will and participation of informed groups and individuals. Through its philosophy of **empowerment through knowledge,** Canada's International Development Research Centre (IDRC) has long believed in the importance of building and maintaining research capacity in the developing world.

This book focuses on some of the scientists and academics who are spearheading research for international development around the world. These women and men represent a small sampling of the host of researchers funded by IDRC over its 25-year history, and, given the calibre of these many researchers, making the final selection of candidates for this book was not easy. In the end, the profiles presented here cover the various geographical regions and some of the assorted disciplines in which IDRC has been involved throughout its history: from environment, health, and medicine, to social and economic policy, to information science, agriculture, and technology; from Benin and South Africa, to the Philippines, Sri Lanka, and Viet Nam, to Chile, Jamaica, and, of course, Canada.

You, the reader, will meet some remarkable and successful individuals within these pages. Here, the researchers tell their stories, ranging from the personal to the professional. The personal stories yield compelling and often moving reminiscences. The professional information and anecdotes serve to show just how extraordinary their achievements are, given the challenges and difficult working conditions for scientific research in Third World countries. You will also meet the local professional journalists who were assigned to research and write these profiles. These individuals were able to put the researcher and his or her work in a context that a foreign writer from abroad could have never achieved.

We occasionally read in the newspapers or hear on television about a scientific advance — such as the malaria vaccine or the family-planning vaccine — that has been achieved by a scientist from Asia, Latin America, or Africa. Yet, most of the interesting and important research going on right now in the Third World is completely unknown to us. New, nonpolluting technologies are being developed; economic and trade policies are being designed and applied; powerful medicinal plants from the rain forests are advancing the cause of medicine and health care; new types of high-yield rice and other crops are being developed. In almost every discipline, there is research happening in the Third World whose results will one day benefit all of the peoples of the world, both South and North. The researchers presented in this book are providing concrete solutions to serious problems in their own part of the world; at the same time, they are also contributing to the world body of knowledge from which we all draw.

With 1995 marking IDRC's 25th anniversary, it seemed appropriate to recognize publicly, in this book, at least some of the outstanding researchers whom it has been our privilege to know and support. We hope that these profiles amply illustrate that sustainable development arises from the needs and abilities of people themselves, and that empowering people with knowledge and opportunities for personal and professional growth is key to a healthy and sustainable future worldwide.

Keith A. Bezanson
President
International Development Research Centre

Eusèbe Alihonou
(Benin)

*P*hysician and professor Eusèbe Alihonou believes that sound minds and bodies build strong nations. Love for Benin has led him to devote his life to community health care and research. As the director of a health research centre and Dean of the Health Sciences Faculty at the University of Benin, he helps to train the next generation of physicians and medical researchers. Alihonou has proven that good health care is not necessarily expensive, but it does require the full and active participation of the community.

by Jérôme Bibilary

"SERVE. FIRST SERVE THE POOREST AND THE MOST disadvantaged." This formula, which may sound trivial at first glance, summarizes the goal and meaning in life for Eusèbe Magloire Alihonou. Hard work and determination have made this native of Benin an exemplary figure in the field of development research.

As his 60th birthday approaches, Professor Alihonou wears a ready smile that may give, at times, a misleading impression of unconcern. In fact, he worries about the situation of the rural poor. "These people lack the bare minimum necessary for existence, and cheap talk is not their style. Rural people suffer from cruel shortages of everything. To make their situation more tolerable, however, they are exhorted to rise above their depression. With this aim, they are showered on every occasion with speeches that fail to teach them how to take concrete action. Words, nothing but empty words, designed always to raise their morale, never to provide them with concrete help. It's not fine words that the peasants need, but concrete actions to solve their problems or prepare the way for future action.

"The comfortable lifestyle, which most African elites enjoy, weaves a soft cocoon around their souls that they are loath to leave. It also restrains them from doing anything more than making demagogic promises. That is why, at a time when the peasants are fighting for the bare minimum, it seemed important to join them and share with them their poverty and their experience. Closer to them, face to face with their problems, it is easier to understand their situation."

This is the path Professor Alihonou chose in dedicating himself to improving the living conditions of the most disadvantaged people, especially those in the countryside. Alihonou is, above all, deeply convinced of the beneficial effects of loving thy neighbour and the virtues of sharing. He feels that solitary happiness is impossible. He also has an unshakable conviction in the potential for spreading greater justice and fairness throughout the world.

There is nothing really surprising in that. Although his parents came from Ouida, one of the first cities founded by the Portuguese on the west coast of Africa, Alihonou was born on 16 December 1938 at Dogbo, in the Department of Mono in southwestern Benin. Living conditions there were far from adequate. Growing up among people of modest means undoubtedly had a positive influence on his subsequent determination to improve their quality of life.

Eusèbe's mother was a midwife who traveled the communities of her native land on a succession of assignments to serve the most disadvantaged classes of society. She was watched by her son, whom she invariably took with her on her travels. In this way, the future physician developed a social conscience and a desire to help others. At Victor-Ballot College in Porto-Novo, where he went to high school, young Eusèbe flourished under the guidance, faith, and rigorous training of his teachers, of whom he still says, with great admiration, were "learned, even if they lacked impressive degrees." Later, he went into medicine and graduated from the University of Dakar.

He returned to Benin in 1971 as a specialist in gynaecology and obstetrics, but this did not seem to satisfy his calling to serve others. "Once I was back in my own country, I started working in the maternity hospital in Cotonou. I was working very hard, but I soon realized that I was actually only caring for a tiny fraction of the population. I concluded that I had to do something that would allow me to help more people. And to achieve this noble goal, I had to leave the hospital.

"I could see that my country was regularly squandering its already limited resources because of inefficient management. To maximize the impact of our meagre resources, we Beninois had to learn to manage them better and choose viable, but less costly solutions. To achieve this, it was necessary to focus more closely on the countryside, where the majority of the population lives and where living conditions are, paradoxically and unfairly, less comfortable than in the cities. This is how I came to work in rural communities."

The die was cast. To help the people among whom he had decided to live, he had to reconcile two objectives: health and development. The logic behind it was elementary: "Someone who does not enjoy good health cannot be productive. And without productivity, there can be no socioeconomic development. Good physical and mental health is a prerequisite of fulfilment, development, and productivity, in short, essential for leading an independent, self-supporting life."

There was one prerequisite for a successful undertaking, however: to find out from people what their needs were, rather than proceeding with unilateral actions that sometimes ultimately prove inappropriate. It was this concern that lay behind the first step: "We began by asking the people what their health problems were. We need roads, they replied, so we can get our pregnant women to health-care centres quickly. We also want to learn to read and write because, if we can read, we will understand many things more quickly on our own and there will be more and more of us who learn about them."

Alihonou admits that he is armed with a certain "weapon" in his struggle — his deep faith in the black race and in the ability of his country, Benin, to contribute something to the international community by using all the means within its grasp. The professor made effective use of this weapon when he established the Health Sciences Faculty at the National University of Benin, which is still the only institution of its type in the country.

Working with Professor Edouard Goudote and Professor Fernand Pignol, a French *coopérant*, he accepted the challenge of setting up the faculty. The project, which was first discussed under a tree in Professor Goudote's garden, seemed quite foolhardy and impossible at that time. It has nonetheless survived its detractors and is today the only part of the university that has no permanent expatriate teaching staff. It has some sixty faculty members, more than half of whom have a master's degree, with many having reached the level of associate professor. Hence the simple statement that underpins everything Professor Alihonou does: "You can do a lot with little, provided you have the determination, courage, perseverance, and expertise." The Primary Health-Care (PHC) Strategy, which led to the famous Bamako Initiative, was designed on the basis of this philosophy. Everything began with a modest project in 1983 in the little village of Pahou, 20 kilometres west of Cotonou: the Pahou Health Development Project.

"We began," recounts Professor Alihonou, "by using, under their generic name, the essential medications for oral rehydration and vaccination recommended by UNICEF [the United Nations Children's Fund] and WHO [the World Health Orgnization]. This enabled us to save an incredible number of children. In 1985, the Benin Ministry of Health incorporated the results of the operation into a national health-care program, which gave birth to the Expanded Vaccination/Primary Health Care Program [known under its French initials as PEV/SSP]. The program was subsequently extended to Guinea and other countries in the West African subregion, and, ultimately, it became the Bamako Initiative, which has continued to flourish because of the confidence the international community finally placed in it. Today, the entire world believes in this initiative, and this has provided all the countries in this part of Africa with public services that are used by an ever-increasing percentage of the population."

Initially set up to implement primary health care in the areas of services, research, and training, the Pahou Health Development Project, after it generated the Bamako Initiative, was rapidly overtaken by its own dynamics. At Alihonou's urging, and in close cooperation with the population it serves, the project's management and research team accordingly expanded the scope of its activities to include the development dimension. In 1989, the project was remodeled into a Regional Health and Development Centre (CREDESA), a tool of economic and social development that uses a multidisciplinary approach involving sociologists, economists, doctors, nurses, midwives, and social workers. One of its key roles is "to train qualified personnel in the areas of health, research, and program delivery, both in terms of consultation and expertise, for Benin and all the countries in the region."

"It is worth stressing particularly," continued Professor Alihonou, "the importance of the training dimension, in which our partners in the developed world are active, specifically the Ford Foundation, the Netherlands Royal Tropical Institute, the International Development Research Centre, and the Canadian International Development Agency. At our request, these institutions agreed to provide scholarships on a regular basis for the young people who help us on this project, and this has enabled us to maintain a satisfactory pace of training. As far as research is concerned, we share the results of our activities with the other countries in the region through UNICEF and WHO."

Parallel to CREDESA, Professor Alihonou has developed a range of other initiatives designed to enhance people's standard of living and, at the same time, promote development. One of these is the Centre for Research into Human Reproduction and Population, which takes over the mission of a family health unit at the Cotonou University Gynaecology and Obstetrics Clinic (CUGO). The main goals of this centre are "childbirth without risk," combatting infertility, and other activities such as the "baby-friendly hospitals" initiative. CUGO, which Alihonou founded and directs, employs four professors, six doctors, forty medical residents, and a hundred other medical staff, including midwives and nurses.

It is impossible to grasp the full range of Professor Alihonou's initiatives without some idea of what researchers in developing countries do. He, himself, put it clearly and succinctly: "Researchers in the South must focus on finding solutions to problems that obstruct the improvement in living conditions in their country. They must conduct operational research and action research. In other words, their research must find solutions to problems that hamper development. The best of these solutions are tested under experimental conditions and the results are evaluated."

Eusèbe Alihonou advocates the establishment of a network of relationships between researchers in the North and in the South, with the aim of using the ensuing interdependence as a springboard for enhanced mutual awareness: knowing people better to serve them better. Researchers in the South must, however, climb down from the pedestal onto which their degrees have hoisted them and agree to learn, even from contact with younger, more junior colleagues. This is one of the keys to the many successes achieved by the Director of CREDESA. There are, of course, many others, such as the mechanisms he institutes to ensure the durability of his projects. Three of CREDESA's mechanisms deserve special mention.

First, the centre develops its research findings as soon as possible, turns them over to the appropriate program, as defined by the government, or offers them to other countries in Africa. Second, CREDESA trains the human resources it requires for its programs in such a way that they are aware of domestic problems and able to provide expertise to their country of origin and the rest of Africa. Third, the centre makes communities participate in solving their own problems: this participation is understood in terms of a partnership, or, better, in terms of control by the communities themselves of activities carried out to solve problems.

In short, the key lies in the ability to make the tripod of decision-makers, professionals, and communities work on solving a range of problems: setting priorities, choosing solutions, implementing them, evaluating the results, and programing. Hence the necessity for an ongoing dialogue between the three elements of the tripod. The degree of participation by each element in the dialogue depends on the educational level in the communities. Therefore, there is a need to provide schooling for 80 to 90 percent of school-age children. This will endow communities with genuine autonomy in acquiring useful knowledge. For this process to reach fruition, however, there is a 10- or 20-year waiting period before everything functions in a sustained, rigorous manner, with the players involved having adopted a spirit of self-denial and sacrifice. This is seldom easy to achieve.

For Professor Alihonou, it is a question of patience and courage, qualities he possesses in abundance. He is aware of the scope of the responsibilities that rest on his shoulders as each success creates its own new set of expectations and responsibilities. He is already preparing his successors by working side by side with a number of young people trained in top universities, most of whom speak French and English.

Alihonou has boundless faith in the youth of Africa and, in particular, of Benin. He states with genuine confidence: "If you help the young people of Benin, they can succeed. I have fought to provide young people with conditions conducive to acquiring knowledge and they have astounded me."

For all his admiration and belief in them, Professor Alihonou is nevertheless somewhat apprehensive about these young people. He knows that it is a difficult challenge asking young people to make sacrifices to enable future generations to succeed. Yet Alihonou maintains an unshakable faith in the genius of his people. He unhesitatingly cites as an example the peaceful transition of his country from a Marxist dictatorship to a democracy as additional proof of the intelligence and genius of Benin's people.

Professor Alihonou's views on religion are disconcertingly simple. As a practicing Catholic, he is not against other religions, be they Protestant, Muslim, or anything else. Religion is for him an institution that affirms and practices human solidarity. In the name of absolute freedom of conscience, he solemnly declares that he respects the convictions, doctrines, and beliefs of others. He does not acknowledge that any individual who can contribute to improving the lot of the human race can be rejected on religious grounds. With regard to the current crisis in several countries in the region following the collapse of communism and the advent of democracy, Professor Alihonou notes bitterly that, instead of joining forces to search for solutions to the real problems we face, we prefer to engage in sterile invective and arguments that are of no benefit whatever to our countries.

As a former member of the Dakar Federation of Free Students, Eusèbe Alihonou is a staunch advocate of freedom, albeit skeptical of the powerful influence of capitalism. This is part of the reason why the devaluation of the CFA franc causes him serious concern. However, he hastens to add, "This must not be sufficient to snuff out the determination of Africans." On the contrary, the devaluation should provoke a shockwave, spurring the people of Africa to embark on a moral rearmament that will make them capable of choosing paths to development that are appropriate to their culture, although always imbued with humanism and compassion.

This, then, is a portrait of Eusèbe Magloire Alihonou. A good man: optimistic, generous, ever ready to sacrifice himself for others. One colleague says: "He is a man of outstanding stature and impact, a patriot, blinded by a passion to contribute to the happiness of others and alleviate suffering." This feeling is shared by almost everyone who knows him, for whom the Professor is "love": love and humility. Whatever the verdict about the overall worth of his activities, what is surprising is his astonishing ability to consistently achieve his objectives, with determination, professionalism, and modesty in equal measure. Such a man must be acknowledged as a benefactor to his country.

His only concerns are to improve the living conditions of the rural masses and to hasten Africa's development. Are there any missions more noble?

Jérôme Bibilary is the editor of Benin's monthly newsletter, La Lettre du Gouvernement, *and has published over 300 articles in Benin periodicals.*

PIERRE SANÉ
(Senegal)

*H*ead of Amnesty International, Pierre Sané was born in Senegal and educated in Africa, France, England, and Canada. He is a true internationalist with a broad education in political science, economics, and business, and a commitment to improve the respect for human rights worldwide. He is both an intellectual and a man of action. Being an African conscious of the history of his continent has given him a horror of oppression and a determination to find solutions to problems of underdevelopment.

by Jean-Pierre N'Diaye

CHESTNUT VENDORS APPEAR ON EVERY STREET CORNER and the Paris sky glows a joyful blue. Nature, reborn, is celebrating in the cheerful, relaxed atmosphere generated by a sun so warm it is more reminiscent of cities in the South.

Here at the airport I await Pierre Sané, whom I have never met, but who is arriving from Geneva and who will be departing Paris tomorrow for London. Surveying the crowd of hurrying passengers in the corridor, I notice a man's shape, medium height, a purposeful look, athletic, carrying a big, heavy black bag around his shoulders, supported by his right arm, like a Touareg nomad. In his other hand, the man carries an equally heavy, large briefcase that balances him in his rapid movements. The sight of him reminds me of prominent lawyers who, striding up the courthouse steps toward the court room, reflect the seriousness of the cases they are defending by the look of alert determination in their eyes and the weight of the files they are carrying. Pierre Sané is clearly on a mission.

As Secretary General of Amnesty International, based in London, Sané is called upon to travel to all parts of the world where torture, arbitrary imprisonment, kidnappings, and disappearances organized by governments and armed opposition gangs are routine.

It is not by accident that an African heads Amnesty International. Africa is one region of the world that desperately needs Amnesty International to provide voice and representation to those who have no voice, no power, no connections, and no hope. Amnesty is a cause that has found support in the developed world. It has 1 million members, 90 percent of whom live in just two regions: North America and Western Europe. Pierre Sané says he is willing to work 70 hours a week in this cause if necessary, as this is a battle that is necessary for the entire world, and especially crucial for Africa.

As Amnesty's chief spokesperson, he meets several times with heads of state and senior officials. He goes to meetings and, before the eyes of these very powerful leaders, puts out on the table basic details about victims in that country and their situations: places of detention, locations of torture chambers, pictures of mass graves. The gulf can be immense in meetings such as these, the face-to-face confrontation terrible; it takes strong nerves and a spirit driven by unwavering conviction. Pierre Sané is a fighter.

At first glance, one would not suspect this. Sané has a warm human quality that allows him to talk easily with others regardless of race, class, gender, culture, and religion. He is an attentive listener; he misses nothing. In conversation he creates a kind of "mental tension" at times, yet can just as easily break suddenly into a broad smile to create a moment of relaxation and lightness.

Beside this tireless campaigner for human rights stands wife Ndèye, who comes from a Muslim family and is a history teacher. Together, she and Pierre have two children aged 9 and 13 years. Ndèye comes from Saint-Louis du Senegal, the first city in West Africa. Saint-Louis has acquired a legendary reputation for its cool climate and its hospitality, or *taranga*. Intelligent, refined, and smiling, Ndèye combines tradition and modernity with an innate ease of manner.

Sané has a solid education to his credit, acquired on three different continents. He has an MBA from the Ecole Supérieure de Commerce at the University of Bordeaux in France, an MSc in politics from the prestigious London School of Economics, and has completed the coursework for a doctorate in political science from Carleton University in Canada. This variety of schooling has provided him with a rich, interdisciplinary approach to understanding the world. His training stems from a genuine desire for answers and knowledge, fired by the ambition to put the world right. The combination of interrelated disciplines enables him to have a global and multisectoral vision of the world economy, to measure the impact of its weaknesses and imbalances, and to replot the axes of a new structure.

He says he cannot live passively and contentedly, merely managing the world as it is, with its wounds and its innumerable victims in every corner and on every continent. This is a man with passion and social responsibility. What has shaped these qualities in Sané?

He comes from a continent that has suffered for 400 years from the most ferocious inequalities in its relationships with the rest of the world. Being an African has also given him a horror of oppression and a stubborn determination to find the key to the problem of underdevelopment.

Pierre Sané was born in Dakar in 1948 to a family that came originally from Casamance, a part of southern Senegal where resistance to colonial domination in West Africa lasted longest. His father, Nicolas Sané, was a journalist and trade unionist. Pierre's political education, however, came primarily from his godfather and paternal uncle, especially during the many long Sunday card games. His uncle belonged to the newly formed Radical Party (the PRA-Senegal), which, after fighting for independence, found itself in opposition once the battle had been won. As a child, Pierre repeatedly witnessed the arrests of his uncle. His mother was principal of a technical college for women, and also active in Catholic women's associations working for the emancipation of women. She taught Pierre that the voluntary sector is the crucible of social change, and that volunteerism is a dimension of progress. No lasting progress can be achieved without some minimal self-sacrifice, she would say.

After considerable experience in the private sector, both in France and in Dakar, Pierre opted for a job with a Canadian organization, the International Development Research Centre, which has a regional office in Dakar. He began work there as financial controller.

Why did he choose a Canadian institution, given the wide variety of major, well-established development agencies he might have joined? IDRC offered Pierre Sané freedom of action; as well, it was an organization whose unique ideals he very much shared. In this regard, he readily acknowledges that "the experience gained during these years is the key to my life." He was, in fact, able to compile a comprehensive picture of the basic problems facing Africa by traveling through all the countries on the continent and keeping in constant touch with academics, researchers, and educators. IDRC was an ideal environment for him.

IDRC, since its inception in 1970, has funded applied scientific research aimed at solving problems in the developing world. Its approach is not to impose research programs or offer "turnkey" results, but to treat host-country researchers as indispensable partners, completing their training and giving them full latitude in their research fields. IDRC believes that only research conceived and conducted by local researchers can be useful in building the foundation for sustainable development.

After promotion to Regional Director of IDRC's West Africa office, Pierre Sané led an IDRC mission to South Africa in 1987 to develop a policy of support to independent research. Working with researchers close to the African National Congress (ANC), IDRC formulated a program of research support in economics, and in the fields of urban policy, health, and education. It is hoped that the findings and policy advice of this program now informs the programs of the democratic, postapartheid government of South Africa.

Following his return from South Africa, Pierre Sané was absolutely certain of one thing: "I am returning from South Africa with the firm conviction that this country will soon make an incalculable contribution to the world. By resolving the contradictions that exist in the country, its leaders will overcome those problems that generate race and class conflict. This has not occurred in the United States, but I believe that it will in South Africa. The merciless repression practiced in South Africa gave birth to a resistance movement of the highest quality, and the value of those men and women whom I met is simply outstanding."

The 15 years he spent in direct contact with the hard realities of life in Africa led Pierre Sané to reflect on the complex nature of the concept of development and to formulate a diagnosis. His initial finding: African governments, after 1960, have continued to operate within the confines of an economic system inherited from the colonial model. Today, they are in contradiction with the aspirations of African societies for greater freedom, initiative, and well-being. The primary requirement for progress is to liberate grass-roots creative energies.

With this in mind, Sané became a founding member of PANAF. Its role is to establish in stages, a Pan-African community equipped with a single political entity to allow the free circulation of goods, people, and services. The first goal is to achieve regional integration involving communities that have regained their freedom of initiative. This freedom has today been appropriated by governments that operate solely for the benefit of an oligarchy.

Sané talks about "deconcentration," "decentralization," and "democracy." What West Africa needs, he says, are policies that will promote small- and medium-sized industry. Education and research must be harnessed to serve these businesses by enabling them, among other things, to fine-tune their objectives. The establishment of this industrial fabric can occur only under the aegis of a sound legal and judicial system, in which laws are obeyed and offenders punished.

"Beyond all the fine speeches, the rule of law in a country is judged on the evidence of its practice," says Sané. Government must accordingly rediscover its role as organizer for the benefit of the whole community, in an economy that is moving forward. Education, instead of promoting the self-reproduction of unproductive power elites, must help producers and ordinary citizens. This type of goal presupposes the emergence of an intelligent, ambitious, and responsible elite. The ultimate hope for lifting West Africa out of the rut is the establishment of a community of small- and medium-sized businesses, controlled by the businesses themselves. They will need to organize themselves financially and legally. Their organizational power will force the government to be receptive to the need to orient education and research to achieve economic growth.

Pierre Sané's experience has shaped him into one of the leading actors on the subject of development and human rights. He has committed himself wholeheartedly to spreading awareness of this fundamental link. This relationship is now central to ongoing discussions in major international agencies that are studying the ways and mechanisms of promoting it.

It was while he worked at IDRC as regional director that his commitment to human rights grew. He became an active member of Amnesty International in 1988. Four years later, in 1992, he was selected from 1 200 candidates to lead the organization's impressive program.

What is unique about Amnesty International is its success in mobilizing, through 1 million volunteer members, world public opinion in the defence of human rights. This voice, emanating from many sources, has an undeniable impact: it is irritating, embarrassing, tenacious, and credible. The attacks launched against it testify to its impact. At the head of an organization that has become a channel for receiving all the world's dissonant voices, and armed with the experience he has acquired in Africa — his own continent, and one that is presented throughout the rest of the world as the homeland of despair — the tone is new and the angle of attack, penetrating.

The Third World ceased to exist with the end of a bipolar world. There are now only the rich and the poor, and the dividing line cuts right through the most advanced nations. The concept of the nation state needs rethinking. The nation state, fractured and shaken by the sudden, brutal disappearance of a bipolar world, is caught in the worldwide flows of economic globalization. As far as the developing countries are concerned, the myth of a homogeneous one-party state as the well-spring of an evolving society and economy is bankrupt. As a result, violence is no longer the preserve of the state. It has spread through armed groups that can cause states to explode: this, in turn, obliges organizations such as Amnesty International to focus their actions.

Sané attacks head-on the ideological manipulation practiced by some governments that, to anchor their financial power through the accelerated development of the country, subject the entire population to inhumane conditions. Even more effectively, using arguments that he takes from the source of the religions and philosophies of different civilizations, he dismantles and demolishes the specious pretext of "cultural specificity," as incompatible with democracy and human rights. In other words, the idea that these values are exclusively Western.

On this point, the famous Korean Democrat Kim Doe-Jung, who is known throughout Asia and who has continued his resistance for the past quarter century despite arrests and death threats, supports Sané unconditionally: "Asiatic thought has espoused values that coincide with democracy. In Korea, the founder of the *Tonghak* religious movement identifies Man with Heaven and states that one must serve the former as one serves the latter. The roots of democracy and respect for human rights exist in both the Western and Asian traditions. The great difference is that Europe has managed to forge them into a social system."

Pierre Sané repeats the same ideas in analyzing the cultural basis of African thought. He repeats loud and long: "The assertion that some human rights — the right to a decent life, the right to freedom — are cultural values that are specific only to certain groups is tantamount to dividing the human race into categories. An attitude of this kind is pure racism."

To build itself, to avoid self-destruction, Africa needs solid ethical foundations that transcend the ethnic and religious divisions that are exploited by dubious interests. To now, power has been based on human exploitation, an iron rule, of which Africa has felt the full weight. If it attempts to follow on this path, Africa will always trail behind the other continents.

In talking about "Afro-pessimism," Sané foresees an analogous fate: "Africa is a continent in the process of inventing itself. South Africa will become a peaceful, multiracial society; a moral example to the rest of the world. West Africa will flourish tomorrow. The resources exist in Africa itself, all that is necessary is to mobilize them productively. The world has rid itself of slavery and colonialism; the last empires are crumbling. The days have gone in which men, women, and children were deprived of their dignity and existential aspirations in the name of civilization, progress, religion, and the idea of greatness."

Jean-Pierre N'Diaye has written extensively on human-rights issues and, from Dakar, is a regular contributor to Le Monde, Jeune Afrique, *and* Afrique Nouvelle.

LALA STEYN
(South Africa)

Born into a white, middle-class family in South Africa, Lala Steyn has enjoyed a relatively privileged upbringing, but she has used her advantages to help others. Social researcher and activist, she and her team have worked on gathering information for communities threatened with land eviction. She looks forward to the building of a new South Africa — one that provides equally for all its citizens — and hopes to contribute personally to that new society through her work, her writing, and her role as a mother.

by Zubeida Jaffer

IN THE YEARS WHEN SOUTH AFRICA'S BLACK POPULATION was declared "surplus" and ordered moved to reserves, Lala Steyn was a youngster growing up in one of the white neighborhoods in Cape Town. She was unaware that one day her work as a social researcher would lead her to confront the bulldozers sent to forcibly remove some of these black communities.

Instead, she regularly attended the Dutch Reformed Church in Rondebosch where, with her parents, she rubbed shoulders with some of the grand architects of apartheid. "We went to tea at Vorster's house; it was just a normal thing," says the 33-year-old Steyn as we sit in a room dominated by a diaper bag and a carry cot for her 3-week-old son. "My father was a judge, and he was part of the establishment at the time. We had no little with black people." Vorster was Willem Vorster, one of the chief proponents of apartheid — a man whose government adopted a policy that, over the past three decades, resulted in 3.5 million "Bantu" being forcibly removed from their places of birth.

By the time she reached high school, Steyn became slightly more aware of what was happening. The English Society at the prestigious Westerford High School invited the coloured poet Adam Small to read his poetry in 1976 — the turbulent year when black school children protested against the use of Afrikaans in their schools. Steyn remembers that the state security police visited the principal after the incident and this gave her some inkling that something was going on in the country. "But 1976 came and went without my knowing what was going on," she said.

Little could she have imagined then that a decade later — 11 years later to be precise — she would stand trembling in front of a bulldozer not knowing what to do. A week after she joined the Surplus People Project (SPP) in April 1987, a cry for help came from a community of shack dwellers living in the white group area of Noordhoek, a corner of the Cape where sea, white sands, and green mountains flow together. As researcher and field worker for the project, Steyn was sent to help. She watched in the pouring rain as church ministers prayed for the white landowner to find the strength to tell the police not to move the local people. "They put their hands on the landowner who just stood there saying you have to leave now. He was a tall old man, the white landowner. I can still see his grey hair, his grey face, with stooped shoulders, stooping more and more as the day went by."

By then her gradual transformation from a school-girl to a community activist had come full circle. From never having had contact with black people, she taught herself to communicate with ease with people of different races and backgrounds.

Looking back, she believes that, although her parents were part of the establishment, they gave her the basic human values that were to stand her in good stead. "We had no little with black people, but they gave me the foundation that enabled me to go beyond a racist viewpoint," says Steyn. Her father, Jan Steyn, did move in a different direction after the 1976 uprisings. He left the bench to become involved in the establishment of the Urban Foundation, an organization with a commitment to social change initiated in response to the uprisings.

Her first contact with black people came in 1980 when she joined an organization during her first year at university. POLSTU (the Political Student Union) based at the University of Stellenbosch, which was considered to be a liberal Afrikaner institution in the Cape, was to provide her with the first opportunity to meet compatriots from across the colour line. "We met students from Soweto. I started realizing that things were not right."

She was also exposed then to some of the critical Afrikaner thinkers of the time — such as André duToit and Johan Degenaar — and they challenged traditional Afrikaans thinking, urging her on to pursue her studies in philosophy to the honours level, "which qualified me for nothing." But she had firmly become part of *"die andersdenkende tradisie"* (the tradition of those who thought differently).

The ease with which she ventures into unknown homes today is a skill that developed in her student days at the University of Stellenbosch. It was the early 1980s — a time when students were inclined to move off campus into communities to express their social commitment. She remembers going from door to door in the poor communities surrounding the university to raise public awareness of the shortcomings of the tricameral (three-level) parliamentary system that the government was about to introduce. She laughs as she recalls that the people were not always interested to find her at their doors. "Sometimes they did not want to be disturbed from their television."

Those days were clearly formative for Steyn. "I joined the United Women's Organization and got to know local women from the coloured and African areas. The greatest experience came with the United Democratic Front's [UDF] million signature campaign." The UDF was a major political movement established in 1983 to oppose apartheid, and it brought together local organizations such as the women's organization that Steyn belonged to.

A further deepening of her communication skills with local people came the following year when she joined the teaching staff of Luckhoff High School in Stellenbosch. She taught English as a second language to the predominantly coloured Afrikaans-speaking scholars. "I joined the school because I was looking for a way to help contribute to change," says Steyn. "I learned a lot from the kids. I had to find ways to make English more accessible and language more simple."

She left the school at the end of that year to marry her university love, lawyer Dawie Bosch. Both she and Bosch shared a commitment to the empowerment of rural populations and they chose to work in the rural town of Montagu, north of Cape Town, where they established an Afrikaans literacy program for farm workers. Their efforts at finding ways to make language accessible were to be of great benefit to her in the years that followed.

On the farms and surrounding areas of those mountain valleys, life went on as usual despite the great upheavals in the country. Those were the years of the states of emergency when thousands were detained, tortured, and shot in the streets. It was a difficult time for Steyn and Bosch. As a lawyer, Bosch soon shifted to running an advice office to assist workers in the nearby black location of Zolani. Their work attracted the attention of the local security police and they were followed and watched. They lived on the border of the coloured and white area in a house occupied by staff members of the project. "We were racially mixed and the white neighbours did not like us." The neighbourhood where she lives today is not segregated and she is relieved that her sons will be growing up in a racially mixed community barely 10 kilometres from where she herself was raised.

The pressure on her husband to do military service forced Steyn to leave Montagu and led her to join SPP. As with a number of young white South African males, Bosch was expected to do 2 years of compulsory service in the army. He applied for alternative service as a conscientious objector and was eventually placed at the city council in Cape Town. "Dawie's father, who was a Christian minister, had to go to Bloemfontein to testify to the special court that his son was a pacifist and religious," explains Steyn. Bosch's efforts to be placed in the rural town of Worcester failed, and the two moved to Cape Town.

It is cold and rainy outside, not unlike the day when she first faced those bulldozers in Noordhoek. Despite her slight frame, I sense a tremendous strength of purpose as she bends forward to continue her story. Her face tightens and her eyes momentarily lose their sparkle as she describes a scenario that she was to live through many times over in her years as an activist researcher. "We would bring in the press, community leaders, take legal action, and help stay the removals," says Steyn. "In Noordhoek, it worked for up to a year and then the authorities came one night at 3 a.m. and piled the people and their belongings onto trucks at gunpoint."

It became crucial for her to brace herself against the bitter emotions that were to well up in her. She learned to maintain a certain detachment in her work: "I had to cut myself off from too much of a personal relationship with the people." She concentrated her energies on gathering the information needed by the communities to fight for their right to land. She could not fall apart each time she watched entire families being uprooted. This no doubt contributed to her survival and growth as a researcher.

Lala Steyn now manages a team of researchers working toward a community-based strategy for use of agricultural land in the Namaqualand reserves. She is the SPP coordinator of the

Action Research and Documentation Unit, which receives financial support from IDRC.[1]

Namaqualand is a sparsely populated, semidesert area in the northwestern corner of South Africa covering 47 700 square kilometres. It has a population of 60 000 and is made up of fourteen small urban settlements, six "coloured reserves," vast stretches of white-owned land, and mining company property. The reserves were formed during a historical process that deprived Khoi-Khoi tribes of their land. As the Dutch colonialists took the land of these tribes at the Cape, they moved northward to Namaqualand. Two Khoi-Khoi–Dutch wars in 1658–1660 and 1673–1677, and a smallpox epidemic in 1713, destroyed most of the tribes. By 1761, the stock farmers had established themselves in the Kamiesberge near where Leliefontein is today. By 1795 and 1847, the border of the Cape Colony had been moved by the invading colonialists to the Orange River. The indigenous people were effectively driven off their land and grouped into reserves, which started as mission stations to offer a measure of protection against the colonialists.

Africans were, because of apartheid legislation, not allowed to live in Namaqualand except as contract labourers in mine compounds. The only African settlement is in Port Nolloth, where Steyn was to have her first experiences with the people of this vast territory. "With the ending of apartheid, Africans can now live permanently in Port Nolloth. They have been given land."

Availability of land and land usage will continue to remain crucial issues in the years to come. The research coordinated by Steyn challenges development strategies unfolded by the government in the 1980s. It began applying a development strategy that had as its aim the division of communal land in

---

[1] In January 1995, Steyn left SPP to implement a land-reform program in South Africa.

the reserves into economic units for hire to individual farmers. The system was applied in Leliefontein, Steinkopf, and the southern part of the Richtersveld — all three larger reserves. A call for help came from Leliefontein, one of the six reserves in Namaqualand, and thus started Steyn's sojourn into a region of South Africa that is, ironically, second richest in mineral resources while being one of its most underdeveloped areas.

She found that the residents were against the government's plan to sell off economic units to individual farmers. With the assistance of SPP, they applied to the court to set aside the system and won. Yet, after long discussions about the court victories, the communities realized that the government still had the power to implement the economic unity system in a different way. Although the local people had valuable knowledge about land management, they did not have access to technical information from other sources and did not have the skills to document what they knew. Once again, the research unit at SPP stepped in.

SPP appointed a development researcher for 6 months, under Steyn's supervision, to help draw up a management plan for the three reserves where land was being used communally. "While the research offers possible solutions to problems, we did not work out how the management strategy could be applied," says Steyn. "The reason was that communities were still divided and there was then no representative local or central government." With a new government in place, despite her reservations, she has greater hope: "There is a chance to shift policy at last."

Yet the only guarantee of changed policies lies in the participation of ordinary people in formulating development plans. She and her fellow researchers have found the participatory research appraisal (PRA) approach to be most suitable to their development objectives. "We bring together the people in the local community and involve them in the discussion of the issues. This forms an integral part of our research," says Steyn.

In this way, they try to alter community perceptions of researchers. "The difficulty is that researchers extract information, but what do they leave behind? The research must have value for the community. With the PRA approach, the people are involved in developing the plan," says Steyn.

But there are complications here too. "Sometimes, as researchers, we have different positions from the community. But then, we have to accept their decision because we want to avoid top-down policies," she continues. With the negotiation process going on in this country, this has not always been so easy. "Negotiators would approach us and want to know what the people want in this region. Researchers are thus faced with the danger of becoming experts of what the people want and getting more and more removed from the local community."

The greatest challenge for her remains the ongoing empowerment of local people. And this takes time. "If the community is forced to accept quick decisions, they will later retract them. There were times when it was frustrating to answer a question over and over again. But it was necessary to ensure that the agreement arrived at had full community support."

The organization of local communities brought its own problems. SPP opened an office in Namaqualand in an attempt to coordinate the land struggles in the whole region. "The idea was that we would hand over control of the office to the community after 2 years," says Steyn. Those 2 years (1990–1992) were some of the most difficult times for her. "There were internal differences among the communities that made central coordination of the work difficult. We decided to eventually close down the office and have found it better to work at a local level and link up communities when common issues arise." Steyn has also found it useful to draw on the assistance of a wide range of researchers beyond her team to both deepen the understanding of local people and to strengthen their demands.

Demonstrating the changes that are currently underway in South Africa, SPP recently hired a Namaqualand resident, Boeboe van Wyk, to coordinate and lead the land claims struggle. With the support of over fifteen local communities, van Wyk also works very closely with Cape Town SPP workers.

A report on the communal grazing patterns in one of the reserves, the Northern Richtersveld, compiled by researchers from the University of Cape Town, helped inform the negotiation process for the formation of a national park in that reserve. "When stock farmers in this reserve were told that they would have to vacate 162 445 hectares of their land for the formation of a national park, they saw this as another act of dispossession," Steyn told a summer-school university program on Namaqualand: the neglected land. "The people were not opposed to the formation of a park but wanted it on terms favourable to them."

Calling on the expertise of additional researchers meant that environmentalists and other organizations become aware of the situation in the Richtersveld. "This resulted in many valuable contributions being made from outside and inside the country," says Steyn. "Environmentalists such as Richard Hill and Fiona Archer, who believe that the interests of local people and conservation can and should be integrated, played an important role. They made all parties to the negotiations aware of other models of national parks in other parts of the world. They explained to the community what a national park is and can be. In addition, they questioned the assertion that stock farming was the sole cause of overgrazing in the Richtersveld."

Her travels to Bolivia, Brazil, and Chile in 1992 have made her doubt that there will be proper land reform in South Africa. She came away after 2 months with the feeling that land reforms are very difficult. "The lessons of land reforms in these countries were not taken into consideration during the negotiations for a new constitution," Steyn maintains. "We have been limited by the process. We have an interim constitution that protects property rights."

For her, one guarantee for greater reforms lies in researchers working as activists to help strengthen and empower local people in their struggles. The Latin American experience has taught her that there has to be strong local organization. "If there is no strong local organization, the political will to do anything becomes less and less." Believing that action research has contributed to building such organization, Steyn has now turned her attention to passing on her skills to other researchers.

With the momentous changes taking place in the country, Steyn herself is undergoing change. "As the new South Africa is born, I am going through my own transition. I have just had Themba who is 3 weeks old and my firstborn, David, is now 17 months. For years now, I have been traveling into the rural towns regularly, but now I have to find another role for myself. I could never have done it with children."

She expects to be more office bound and to have more time for her children and her husband, who remains committed to the upliftment of South Africa's rural poor. "Dawie works for the Centre for Rural Legal Studies in Stellenbosch. They are developing legislation for farm workers," Steyn says with pride in her voice.

A wealth of experience that many researchers in less turbulent times would have taken a lifetime to acquire, lies within this young energetic woman. The tradition of action research that she remains committed to will be carried through to the young researchers who will train under her. She has lived through the momentous times of this nation: born into a system that made large numbers of her compatriots "surplus people," growing up to help fight this system, and fortunate enough to have witnessed in her lifetime the return of the "surplus people" to their rightful citizenship. This citizenship will only become meaningful through just restoration of land, and Steyn's research tradition — if extended and deepened in the years to come — provides some guarantee this can be achieved for the poor of South Africa.

Zubeida Jaffer, an award-winning journalist based in Cape Town, South Africa, specializes in issues of development and women's rights.

Gelia Castillo
(Philippines)

A specialist in rural sociology, Filipina social scientist Gelia Castillo was an early pioneer in the concept of participatory development. Her ideas have influenced thinkers, policymakers, and decision-makers in government, international development circles, and academe. She has found immense personal satisfaction in a long career devoted to teaching, writing, and travel. Born into a poor family, Castillo credits her achievements to her father's influence: he taught her that hard work and helping others is the sine qua non of a successful life.

by Criselda Yabes

"WHAT'S VERY VERY SIGNIFICANT IN MY LIFE IS THE FACT that we were poor," says Gelia Castillo, recalling her early childhood. At 66 years of age, this social scientist, author, and teacher is retired from academic life and has left an impressive body of work. But it is her early years that left the most indelible imprint on her. "I come from a poor family but life has been good to me, and I shall repay it somehow. That is my philosophy. I join projects and causes that have a direct bearing on people's lives. That is part of what I am, and what I will always fight for."

Her parents were a strong early influence, especially her father, who convinced her that academic achievement would be key to her future. Her father was a government clerk at the public works department; her mother, a cook who sold prepared meals door-to-door and sometimes worked in the kitchens of wealthy families.

Gelia Castillo's family lived in Pagsanjan just outside Manila. The town was a mix of the very rich and very poor. The rich neighbourhoods contained mansions encircled by high walls, and Gelia Castillo recalls as a little girl accompanying her mother through the back gates of these walls to deliver food, and glimpsing a luxurious, extravagant lifestyle. "My mother and I used to take the 'servants' stairs.' Big houses generally had two flights of stairs, one used by the family and their rich visitors, and the other used by servants, domestics, and people like us."

Castillo's family lived in a bamboo hut. A typhoon destroyed their home and they were forced to evacuate along with hundreds of other displaced families, until they eventually resettled and rebuilt.

In her speeches, Castillo frequently touches on the Filipino cultural trait called the *Bayanihan* spirit of mutual help. It is represented in a caricature of ordinary folks carrying on their shoulders a thatched hut held by bamboo poles. Although it is supposed to show that Filipinos help one another in times of hardship, Gelia Castillo says "perhaps it is time we peeled off this romantic image to find out why the house is being moved to another place. Maybe it is because the family does not own the land on which its house sits."

Throughout her career, Gelia Castillo has published extensively. Her subjects range from agricultural school administration to the team approach in community development; from rice to potato farming; from an analysis of the changing social images in a developing society to the "protein gap."

She has written three books: *All in a Grain of Rice*,[1] which reviews the social and economic implications of the new rice technology in the Philippines in the early 1970s; *Beyond Manila*,[2] a vast study on rural Filipino life that was, according to some academicians, the first and most comprehensive of its kind; and *How Participatory is Participatory Development?*,[3] which

---

[1] Castillo, G.T. 1975. All in a grain of rice: a review of Philippine studies on the social and economic implications of the new rice technology. Southeast Asian Regional Center for Graduate Study and Research in Agriculture, Los Baños, Laguna, Philippines.

[2] Castillo, G.T. 1979. Beyond Manila: Philippine rural problems in perspective. International Development Research Centre, Ottawa, ON, Canada.

[3] Castillo, G.T. 1983. How participatory is participatory development? A review of the Philippine experience. Philippine Institute for Development Studies, Makati, Philippines.

deals with the experience of mass participation in developing rural communities.

Beyond Manila is her most famous book. Published by IDRC, it was the first comprehensive work on combining the issues of income distribution, employment, labour, education, and migration. She underscored the definition of a "household," saying that the role of women and children contributes greatly to the dynamics of society.

Relaxing in her home in Los Baños, Laguna, where she was for many years Professor of Rural Sociology at the College of Agriculture, University of the Philippines, Gelia Castillo remembers her father who died 20 years ago. Antonio Tagumpay never went to college, but he made sure his children received an education. Gelia, the third of six children, finished elementary and high school with top honours, and, when she graduated *magna cum laude* with a Bachelor of Arts in Psychology from the University of the Philippines, her father was proud but always pushed her to try harder. "He told me, you have to be the best in school. You have to be far above the rest, because if not, you will be just like them. He was right. If you want to get somewhere, there's no other way. That was the only way."

Although he had only a high school education, her father wrote and spoke English well enough to always help his children with their schoolwork. To pay for his children's school tuition, her father sold a parcel of coconut land he inherited from his father years earlier. Typically, he never broadcast this fact, and it was only recently that Castillo learned about this land sale. Small wonder she has such pride in her father and warm gratitude for the many sacrifices he and her mother made for their children.

On the day of her high school graduation, as she walked to the podium to receive her diploma, she told herself, "One day, I will return to this school as guest ceremony speaker." That meant she wanted the town, her teachers, and classmates someday to recognize her as the girl who succeeded. "My motivation was very strong because of my father. That's why today, I tell my children, you're lucky in a way, the fact that you did not have to go through what my family went through. But it gave me character. It gave me something to strive for."

Gelia Castillo did return, armed with her master's degree in rural sociology from Pennsylvania State University and her doctorate from Cornell University — foreign education rare for anyone of her social background. She has been awarded with several research grants and fellowships from various organizations and universities abroad for projects involving social development. In all, her activities have taken her to forty countries around the globe.

"One person can only do so much, especially if it is performed in an outstanding manner," says Priscilla Juliano, an associate professor at the College of Agriculture in Los Baños. "She [Gelia Castillo] admits to not keeping up with the conventional Western literature, but instead she creates a substantive part of the literature in Philippine rural sociology."

"I've always been independent minded. My friends, especially my foreign friends, always ask me: 'Why are you so direct?' I say, that's the way I was brought up. My father always encouraged me to have a tremendous sense of independence and honesty." She has refused administrative positions all these years because, according to her, "it cramps my style." She feels that having to bear the title "dean" or "chairwoman" or "chancellor" could have derailed her freedom to take a stand on certain issues. "Without that burden, I'm freer to do what I want to do. It makes me more productive. I like what I'm doing now, and I think I can have more influence. Many people could not understand that."

Tracing her career in the field of social science, Gelia Castillo says she is grateful to the former Agricultural Development Council funded by John Rockefeller III. As a Cornell graduate, she began writing research papers that she sent to the Council for comments and critiques. "They took an interest in what I was doing and that's very very important. It was important that somebody took the time to critique my work." In fact, it was not long after this that she was invited to deliver her paper on rural sociology in Dijon, France.

Clifton Wharton, Jr, who was then Vice President of the Council, was instrumental in Gelia Castillo's progress. "I really owe him a lot," she says. He helped open doors that exposed her to the circle of prominent scientists and academicians. Both their families remain special friends. "You see," she explains, "there are foundations that will provide you with money, but very few will give you personal and professional care. The Council was one of the very few. I understand the need for professional guidance, that's why I'm trying to help the younger ones."

"She's a nagger of sorts. She pushes people to do competent work," adds Professor Priscilla Juliano. "She has academic and intellectual independence and a consistent ability to do exceptional academic pieces. Probably this is helped by the fact that she is supported by her husband."

Gelia met her future husband, Leopoldo Castillo, at the University in Los Baños shortly after graduation. She was then teaching psychology, sociology, and American history to high school and college students. One year after they met they were married.

"Pol," as she calls her husband, is an animal nutritionist and now Professor Emeritus of the Institute of Animal Science. Similar to his wife, he is well-known in his field.

At a weekend lunch at the Castillo home, "Doc" Castillo, a bespectacled man with a crew cut, seemed mild-mannered in contrast to his wife's sometimes sudden burst of youthful charm. In between scooping from a bowl of chicken broth, she jokes that people often ask her how she copes with her work and raising a family at the same time. "It's simple — I don't do housework," she smiles, pointing to the household helper going about her work in the kitchen.[4]

Coming from a religious Catholic family, Leopoldo Castillo is a strict disciplinarian whose main priority in life is to maintain family ties. He insists that his children use *opo*, the Tagalog word used to address elders with respect. He never turns down a relative seeking financial help and has a standing offer to pay for the education of any family member wishing to study agriculture. When they were newly married, the couple supported three relatives who lived with them, including Gelia Castillo's younger brother. "We don't forget family obligations," she says. "If we didn't help them they wouldn't have had a life of their own."

The Castillos have three children: Bobby, who is in the glass-etching business; a daughter, Gertrude, works as a travel agent in the United States; and the youngest, Nina, is a sociologist, the only child to follow her parent's academic footsteps. "Each time I finish a degree, my father never fails to express his profound excitement," says Nina, who is 32 years old.

Home life for the Castillos is quiet and unhurried. Leopoldo tends to his fruit orchard while Gelia keeps a small circle of women friends, all of whom were former deans of the University of the Philippines. These women call themselves "The Golden Girls," after the American television show. Gelia relies on their friendships even in helping her settle family problems.

It strikes many people that the Castillos portray the ideal couple: humble beginnings, good education, achievers. "My father," adds Nina Castillo, "was never the typical insecure Filipino macho and my mother would always say she would not have accomplished as much without my father's prodding."

---

[4] It is common in Philippine homes to have at least one domestic helper.

"My husband has always been very supportive and has never had any insecurities about my career," says Gelia. "I never felt as a woman that I was at a disadvantage."

She remembers when, in 1978, the Peru-based International Potato Center invited her to join its Board of Trustees. She was unfamiliar with the technical aspects of the potato industry, and some members were apprehensive about a woman trustee coming from the Philippines. The Chairman, a British biologist, summoned her for a get-together breakfast meeting, the result of which guaranteed her position on the board. "How could they be objecting to you," the Chairman had said, apparently impressed by their meeting. For 6 years, Gelia Castillo was the only female member of the board. She has also served on the board of other international organizations, including the International Development Research Centre, the International Service for National Agriculture Research, and the International Council (now Center) for Research in Agroforestry.

"Affirmative action is necessary because in many countries women are really at a disadvantage. Sometimes I think the feminist movement has only been good to the female professionals; but has it helped the poor women or are we just using the poor women to advance our own case? I know this is unpopular thinking and I notice that each time I say these things I'm no longer invited back to speak to that group again."

Gelia Castillo believes Filipino women are "luckier" than other Asians in that, prior to colonization by the Spaniards for 300 years and by the Americans for 50 years, women held a high status in society. "They were rulers and owned land. Then the Spaniards came and it was kitchen, children, and church for the women. And then came the Americans and it was back to school. My interpretation here is that these three phases in our history have blended, so we're neither this nor that. Our femininity comes naturally, and we are independent at the same time. They cannot push us around."

Still, the plight of Filipino women leaving the country to work abroad — mostly as domestics or prostitutes — causes Castillo great distress. "It is sad and frustrating to have all these women going abroad. They have no dignity. They are treated like slaves, but they still go anyway because their work is their source of livelihood. It pains me to see them at the airports being treated badly by immigration."

In a career spanning more than three decades, everything had been smooth sailing for Gelia Castillo — the recognition, the awards, the accomplishments. If there was anything she considered the lowest point in her life, it was when her youngest child Nina became pregnant at 15 years of age. "I thought I was going to die," she recalls sadly of that family crisis long ago. "I was at the top of my career and everything was going well and then all of a sudden, bang! After that I refused any awards. Why will you give me these things? I asked them. I don't deserve it."

For 2 weeks, husband and wife isolated themselves in their home and wept, wondering how something as painful as that was happening to them. They rebounded emotionally to help their daughter pick up the pieces of her life. Nina Castillo married, but the marriage turned out to be a turbulent one and it was later annuled in church. "I asked myself, God, why us? What did we do wrong? But I thought better. We finally woke up and told ourselves that we have a lot of responsibility."

Family friend Gloria Feliciano recalls how the Castillos tried to repair the damage, but at the cost of allowing their daughter to marry at a young age. "Gelia is a unique kind of person. She's an intellectual yet she can be very down to earth. She's also very liberal in her outlook yet she can be so conservative when it concerns her family." Nina Castillo is now carving out a name for herself at the university, like her mother once did. "But, you know, there are pros and cons to being the daughter of Gelia Castillo," Nina quips.

Recently retired, Gelia has no intentions of spending her remaining years in a rocking chair. "My husband says he would be happy to reach the age of 75 or 80. Me, I want to live to 95, because I'd like to marry again when I turn 90." She laughs and continues teasingly, "maybe to a Swede or a Japanese — they have longer life spans."

Turning serious, she adds, "I never really worry about my age. I don't feel old, intellectually and emotionally. It's important for me to stay intellectually alive." When she sums up the years behind her, she says wistfully, "I did not plan all those things. They happened. All I did was to try my best."

Criselda Yabes has worked as a journalist for Newsweek *and the* Washington Post *in Manila and has covered political and military affairs since 1985.*

HARI GUNASINGHAM
(Sri Lanka)

Sri Lankan-born chemist Hari Gunasingham is one of Asia's leading innovators. One of his inventions, a software that can measure and control processes, is optimizing the tea-manufacturing industry and introducing cost savings and environmentally beneficial improvements. Heading a research and manufacturing company in Singapore is a challenge he relishes, yet he does not rule out a career change at some future date, perhaps even a move to the creative arts. Those who know him are not surprised; they only know that given his brains and talent, he would probably also excel at that.

by Catherine Wheeler

BORN IN SRI LANKA AND NOW LIVING IN SINGAPORE, Dr Hari Gunasingham is a compact man with an intense brown gaze. He is restless — always on the go and rarely seated behind a desk. "Let's put it this way, he is not a meetings-and-memo guy," says one of his colleagues. "He operates on an informal basis and tends to cover a lot of ground."

The son of a diplomat, Gunasingham lived in Washington, Bangkok, and Sri Lanka while growing up. In England at 17 years of age, he obtained a degree in chemistry and a doctorate in analytical science at Imperial College. "Hari was definitely one of my very best students," recalls Dr Bernard Fleet, his professor for 4 years at Imperial College. "He was always full of good, innovative ideas."

After a year with British Petroleum and a postdoctoral fellowship, Gunasingham moved to Singapore, where he taught at the National University for 10 years. In 1988, he won the Young Scientist Engineering Award of Singapore for his work in molecular sensors and instrumentation.

In 1985, he began to develop process-control technology for agriculture industries in developing countries. One of his first projects was the development of a personal computer-based software program to design and control laboratory experiments. This noncommercial prototype was later developed into SYNAPSE, a commercial process-control system.

In 1990, with two of his colleagues from the National University, he took the giant step of leaving the university and starting Eutech Cybernetics, a research and manufacturing facility. "He felt that much of his university research had commercial applications and convinced us to take the plunge into the commercial world," says one Eutech cofounder, Bhaskar Narayanan. "We'd been colleagues for 7 years at that time."

"It takes a great leap of faith to give up a secure academic career and go into business," says Professor Fleet, but Gunasingham just shrugs. "Leaving the university was the next logical step. You go through different phases in life. It was time to try and take our work out into the world."

Eutech Cybernetics now employs about 100 people, including many engineers. A subsidiary company in Sri Lanka with twelve employees was set up to execute a project to optimize the manufacturing of tea. Eutech does business in thirty-five countries. The philosophy behind Eutech Cybernetics was to create and manufacture low-cost instruments for product enhancement and to upgrade traditional industries. One of the first set of industrial applications, funded by IDRC, was the adaptation of software and related sensor technologies to optimize the manufacture of tea in Sri Lanka.

"Being Sri Lankan, I know a little about the tea industry," Dr Gunasingham says. "It seemed like a logical place to apply high technology to a traditional industry."

The tea produced on Sri Lanka's 600 tea plantations is of great importance to the country's economy, but the quality of the product has been declining over the years. Obsolete equipment and traditional processes lead to waste, cost overruns, and environmental damage. The tea leaves are dried in wood-burning ovens, which mostly burn very inefficiently.

Fueling the ovens is leading to significant deforestation and air pollution.

"SYNAPSE, our software monitoring system, optimizes the process by monitoring temperatures," explains Dr Gunasingham. "By ensuring that the fires burn more efficiently, we can conserve trees and cut down on air pollution. You could compare the automatically controlled oven to an efficiently running carburetor." The software not only controls the temperatures of the ovens but also measures moisture levels in different teas and adjusts the speed of the conveyors pulling the tea through the ovens. It will link the control of the withering, rolling, fermentation, and drying processes with an overall management system. SYNAPSE is not just a plant-scale energy system. When fully developed, it will be a full management-information system including inventory control, payroll, record keeping, purchasing, and distribution.

A prototype of SYNAPSE is now installed in one tea factory in Sri Lanka, and Gunasingham hopes to install it in other factories over the next few years. Factories in Sri Lanka will serve as demonstration sites for the transfer of technology to neighbouring tea-growing countries such as India, Indonesia, and Malaysia. They will also be the conduit for transferring the technology to other industries such as food processing, palm oil production, and petrochemicals.

Gunasingham intends to incorporate the technology into new tea-manufacturing equipment. Many Sri Lankan tea factories currently use equipment that is over 100 years old. "It takes time to develop an idea into a prototype and bring it to the market, typically 3 or 4 years," he says. "It's early days yet, but we should see some real results in 1996 or 1997. Between the 600 tea plantations in Sri Lanka and 4 000 in India, there will be a very significant environmental impact if the software is widely used to ensure the ovens burn more efficiently."

The most recent SYNAPSE project involves a group of private-sector companies that will apply the technology to areas of pollution control, resource recycling and recovery, and energy conservation in selected highly polluting industries in the Asia–Pacific Region and in Canada.

Gunasingham and his partners have also developed a growing range of low-cost, high-technology instruments for laboratory work. Increasingly, these instruments are designed for environmental monitoring — a sector that will probably account for a significant amount of Eutech's output over the next 3 years.

Eutech Cybernetics has produced over twenty new products since the company was established — about one product every 3 months. These products include several hand-held laboratory sensors to measure pH, temperature, conductivity, and heavy metal concentrations. Another instrument can quickly measure lead in blood.[1] "We've moved the technology out of the laboratory and into the field, into the hands of novices, where it can have the most impact," he explains.

Gunasingham is also in the process of establishing a joint venture in Canada with his former professor, Bernard Fleet. Fleet holds over ninety patents and has worked with Gunasingham on various projects over the years.

"Hari has played the role of visionary ever since we established Eutech in 1990," says Wong Mun Leong, the company's third cofounder. "He sees concepts that are a few years beyond his time. This is important because it allows our company to position itself and plan ahead: a bit like having a crystal ball. He's also a consensus builder, which is a key skill when structuring a company."

Although the concept of Eutech Cybernetics was his and he generated many of its early ideas, Gunasingham is a natural team player. "I think the United Kingdom moulded him more than any other country," says Bhaskar Narayanan. "He was very

---

[1] It is currently undergoing clinical trials supported by the Centres for Disease Control in Atlanta, Georgia, USA.

influenced by the concept of team comradeship. His biggest achievement has been to take his vision and not try to fulfil it alone, but to build a team around it. Because he has so many ideas all the time, he initiates things, delegates, and moves on. He doesn't like to be seen as an individual because basically everything at Eutech is done as a team.

"Hari doesn't seek glory for himself or keep secrets. And he is not a man who tries to run everything himself. He lets people with ideas carry them out freely."

Gunasingham is recognized as one of Asia's leading innovators, and a large factor in his success has been his ability to constantly improve on existing technology. "Do not waste time reinventing the wheel," he urges. "Use that energy to improve on what exists already: incremental innovation. Innovation itself is a creative process, but also a very systematic one. It can be learned. You can train to be an innovator just as you can train to become an artist. You do not have to be a born genius."

His ability to cultivate strategic alliances with major players in the field, such as IBM, AT&T, Matsushita, Hewlett Packard, and Cole Parmer, has proven to be a plus. These companies find that their size makes them unwieldy and inflexible in innovation, and joining with small research and development firms such as Eutech Cybernetics provides them with technical solutions.

"Dr Hari Gunasingham is a brilliant, shy entrepreneur," states Dr Randy Spence, the director of IDRC's Asia office in Singapore. "He has brought together development and technology in a unique way. Hari's is the first project of this kind that IDRC has been involved in. It has taught us a lot and, to some extent, defined a new direction for IDRC in these rapidly changing times."

Gunasingham doesn't fit the usual mould of a person working in the development field. But, having been born in Sri Lanka and traveled extensively, he has an affinity for developing countries.

What does Gunasingham feel about his role in the development of high technology in this developing region? "I don't think of it as a 'role,' nothing so grand as that. I'm just one of the players," he says with typical modesty. "I feel strongly that technology is about knowledge and its utilization, rather than about technology per se. Everyone knows Asia is experiencing tremendous resurgence, both economic and in its huge, well-educated workforce. Technology is very labour intensive, and Asia's workers are well suited to knowledge-based industries. Asia will take giant strides in the next decade. So development in Asia is going to be knowledge-based and less capital intensive."

Previously, there were many advantages attached to a high level of capital investment, which made it possible to enter a particular field. Dr Gunasingham sees danger in continuing this trend. "High capitalization can be a disadvantage because things constantly change these days, and there is a problem of purchasing old technology. In the field of chemistry alone, knowledge doubles every 5 years. It's impossible to keep up. From now on, the investment will be in knowledge."

He does not feel that Western companies are dominating the development of high technology. "The idea that any nation or group of people can dominate the industry is less and less possible. These days, anything developed in the laboratory is in the public domain within a few years. By the start of the next century, it will be very diffused. One of the good things about the information age is the increasing availability of information to virtually anyone who has the means to access it. With electronic mail and other forms of modern communication, it is easy to share information quickly — and harder to prevent its dissemination.

"Personally, I am trying to do something different, be creative, to be happy, to be productive. What I'm doing now is just one area that has proven fruitful. I could easily change my attention to something else in the next few years, turn in a whole new direction. I've always had a desire to go into the creative arts."

Sustainable development is a favourite subject. "I think I can make a greater contribution to sustainable development through the private sector than I could working for a non-governmental organization," he says. "I'm a great proponent of sustainable development. We are at the threshold of a great change in Asia. By the next century, the whole of Asia will be transformed. It has a population of 2.5 billion people, which is growing not only in size, but also in terms of economic power.

"There will be a lot of pitfalls and other difficulties, so donor organizations and others investing in the region must understand the thematic changes and become leading agents for guiding this change. To be an agent of change, your model must be one of sustainable development. I would say that the corporate vehicle is a very good vehicle for sustainable development because it is efficient, not wasteful. Profit as 'capitalist and bad' is now an outmoded concept. In the knowledge-based world, profit is simply the final result of how well you manage your operation. It has nothing to do with exploitation. In fact, in knowledge-based industries, it's the employees who have the real power. Companies go to great lengths to motivate and keep their employees.

"The models have changed. The old Marxist idea of the proletariat is completely outmoded, it's finished. In this new environment, there is a tremendous opportunity for donor agencies to lead. And it's happening already, and it's paying dividends."

Despite a 6-day work week, Gunasingham claims that he never needs a holiday. "A holiday as a logical break from work is alien to me. It's not so much that I enjoy my work, but I'm continually exploring my ability and understanding of the world and applying what I have learned. So what would I do on a holiday: rest, enjoy myself? I do those things in my normal day."

Although his mother tongue is Tamil, he doesn't speak it well. English is the language in which he is most comfortable. "I tried to learn German while I was working there, but I'm very bad at languages."

Having moved around so much when he was young has given Gunasingham a very global perspective. "I have no national preferences. I can fit comfortably into any environment, except that I don't like the cold! Traveling widely has helped me see both sides of an issue. For example, when I lived in Sri Lanka, there were race riots. In England and the United States there were racial problems as well. It was a very formative experience for me. In the States, Afro-Americans were just coming out of their shells. As a young Asian I could see the situation from both perspectives. I could see the fear of the whites, the fear of the unknown, and the anger of the blacks. It's improved a lot over the years, but the problems are very complex. Take Sri Lanka: there's no easy answer, no right or wrong."

A family man, Gunasingham balances the demands of a new business with the needs of his wife and two daughters, 5 and 10 years old. The elder child is in the gifted program at a Singapore school. "Perhaps we have another scientist there," he muses. Years ago, he played the cello, sitar, and veena (a South Indian instrument) and painted. Now there is little time for hobbies except tennis, which he learned 2 years ago. "I am very competitive in sports," he confesses. "And I like American humour, an influence of my early years in the United States. But I never seem to find time to watch the television anymore."

Gunasingham continues to play his role as visionary-in-residence, contributing his own ideas and creating an atmosphere in which others can create and develop their own ideas. His aspirations? "I want to do something useful and interesting, overcome my limitations, improve my knowledge, try to be creative, and do things that are of some use and can be applied to make life easier and better for people." He pauses. "I suppose the real goal is to improve yourself and in the process improve the world around you."

Catherine Wheeler, from her Singapore home, reports on the Canadian business community in Southeast Asia, produces a quarterly newsletter for the Canada–ASEAN Centre, and writes supplements on regional economies for the Financial Post.

JAI KRISHNA NIGAM
(India)

After training in textiles research as a young man, Jai Krishna Nigam branched out into industrial research in his native India, becoming a tireless advocate for "needs-based" research and for closer links between research and industry. Improved productivity is vital to a nation's economic performance and he argues that scientists can play a key role in technological cooperation and indigenous capacity for technology development.[1]

by Ritu Bhatia

As the dynamic director of the Shriram Institute of Industrial Research (SRI) in New Delhi, Dr Jai Krishna Nigam has gained wide respect for creating an independent, self-supporting research institute — a rarity in developing countries — that serves the needs of more than 3 000 industries in India. SRI is a prime model of how industrial research benefits industry and society.

Nigam's own field of specialization is synthetic fibre technology: he is the author of 120 papers and holds some thirty patents. His career has taken some remarkable twists and turns, starting with the doctorate he earned from the University of Leeds and the beginnings of an industrial career abroad, interrupted when fate intervened in the form of a chance meeting with Indira Gandhi.

She told Dr Nigam: "Why are you wasting your time here? Whatever you are doing here, you should be doing it back in your own country. India needs you. I don't think your place is in Europe or the United States." Nigam asked what would happen if he was unable to get a job, but Mrs Gandhi assured him that she would arrange everything once he was back.

---

[1] This profile was prepared just prior to Dr Nigam's untimely death on 13 November 1994. His contribution and commitment to development research is sorely missed.

The memory of this incident brings a smile to Dr Nigam's face. "She said, 'you just come back, and what happens later will be my responsibility.' Without thinking I chucked everything and rushed back to India. I had a PhD, 10 000 pounds [sterling], and plenty of ideas." Of course, another reason for the move was to marry Jaya, a computer scientist he had met at Leeds, who had finished her course and was back in India.

On returning to India, Nigam found the employment situation disheartening. "There were no decent jobs available, so I tried to see Mrs Gandhi, but my attempts were futile; she was inaccessible. Eventually, I rejoined my old employers, J.K. Synthetics."

The next 2 years were an exciting period of learning and growth for Nigam. A transfer from the manufacturing department into research gave him the opportunity to learn new processes. "I had been a fibres person until then, but the research department exposed me to the backward integration of processes: from fibre production, to raw material, and then to chemicals." He was elated when he discovered an improved, cost-saving process. He brought the new technique to the management's attention but, to his astonishment, they were opposed to the idea. "It wasn't worth their while to incorporate my ideas, the savings were too insignificant. Nobody was interested in the long-term gains."

Disillusioned, he quit the company. Fifteen years later, subsequent experience has only reinforced his earlier opinion that "many of our industries in India are bogged down by domestic and conventional issues, by financial and marketing problems, because they focus on short-term objectives to the detriment of technology development and improved productivity, which are vital to a nation's performance. Government, industrialists, and policymakers are not particularly interested in getting involved in technology upgrading because their primary interest is immediate profit generation. But, take it from me, no amount of modernization is going to cure Indian industry of its ills. Indians must do it themselves. Technologies have to be generated, modified, adapted, and updated by Indians."

The inability or unwillingness of industrial concerns in India to develop their own technologies is the main reason for their dependence on imported technology, says Nigam. Because technologies developed by local research institutes do not conform to quality standards, imported technology has become a way of life. He predicts that this trend will continue into the 21st century because the infrastructure for technology development has still not been created within the country.

"Although Indian industry's technological base has advanced considerably over the years, its capacity to generate technology from within has remained limited. Local production has increased in the past three decades, and has replaced some imports, but indigenously developed technologies contribute only marginally to the economy. This is because commercially viable technologies are not being generated by either the private sector, national laboratories, or the universities. The lack of interaction between labs and industry, and poor technology transfer between Indian firms, are other problems we face."

Another reason industrial development has suffered in developing countries is that scientists are not respected or valued. "As long as scientists and technologists remain in the back seat of any industry, that industry will never reach the top. While Indian scientists, doctors, and technicians achieve distinctions in almost all the advanced countries, our technological level inside the country is poor. Scientists and technologists in India are given very little importance. Very few people choose to do research because the career incentives are very low compared with finance or law. Naturally, the outcome of uninterested, unmotivated researchers can only be mediocre work.

"By comparison, Japan and the United States have progressed rapidly because of the incentives these societies offer to their scientists. India has no large corporate sector to champion technology development as a profitable commercial activity. Technology development is not a one-man show and, unfortunately, in India, the spirit of team work and collective activity is missing."

Should developing countries import technology from their more developed counterparts? According to Nigam, "the time gap between international entry and introduction in India for any product used to be two to three decades, but that is continuously widening. Such technology gaps can hardly be bridged by indiscriminate technology imports.

"Today, developed countries are moving into more sophisticated, high-tech areas that are not relevant for developing countries. The result is that the technology gaps are increasing, the difference between the rich and poor is widening. To spread the benefits of technology to the widest range of people, there must be greater technological cooperation amongst scientists beyond the boundaries of any nation; we need to reduce the international barriers that inhibit the benefits of technologies from creation to dissemination. This might seem a fantasy, but as far as I'm concerned it's the only approach possible if we want a uniform spread of basic human requirements globally."

In 1979, Nigam accepted the job of Director of SRI. The establishment of this institute in 1950 was considered a bold and pragmatic venture on the national scientific front and was pioneered by Lala Shri Ram, who was convinced that India could — and must — catch up with the most advanced countries of the world.

However, the institute was in disarray when Nigam took over. The laboratories, systems, and technologies were outdated, the scientists were demoralized, the entire approach was conservative. Nigram was told that, if the institute could not be turned around, it would have to be disbanded. What began as a job quickly became a personal challenge. "It was all very well," he says, "to call the institute self-supporting, but there was no work and no money. Without funds nothing could be achieved."

Nigam immediately made fund-raising a top priority. Next, he began visiting various industrial concerns with the idea of identifying their needs. "I went from one company to the next, to find out what we could do for them. It became clearer every day to me that industry didn't need research. Its immediate needs were analytical services, and information."

With the idea of catering to industry's specific requirements, Nigam set up various departments within the institute. When the problems of environmental pollution became apparent, an environment group was established; the health hazards created by chemicals prompted the institute to create a toxicology unit; and so on. Nigam then proceeded to give total autonomy to the staff. "Whoever was in charge of a particular department was to be a manager. We would identify the job that needed to be performed, and they were in charge of executing this. The institute would provide all the funds. The condition was that they would provide a return on investment."

Nigam is currently President of the World Association of Industrial and Technological Research Organizations (WAITRO), an international forum for research and technology organizations throughout the world, which aims to promote the exchange of information on emerging technologies and skills. "Through interacting with international organizations I became aware of the importance of research institutes in the most developed industrial societies," he says. "Rather than wasting time on repetitive technology development — which is what poorer, developing nations do — I realized that these institutes played a crucial role in providing scientific services that fulfil industrial requirements, whether that be analytical or environmental services, or providing information. These institutes have been effective in developing local expertise, developing technology suitable for local conditions, as well as evaluating new international technologies and adapting them to local requirements. If the services offered by these institutes are availed of, industrial growth can be accelerated."

Nigam's emphasis on "needs-based" industrial research has transformed the Shriram Institute into a vibrant, growth-oriented organization. From a meagre budget of 3.5 million Indian rupees per annum in 1980, the institute's current annual budget is about 60 million rupees (around US $2 million), through its own earnings, and with no increase in its staff strength.

The institute offers its services to private and public industry alike. Today, about 20 percent of the total activity at the institute is research and development based. "We do research as a contract laboratory for those who don't have the infrastructure to do their own research. If we focused only on research and development, we would interact with the industry only five times a year. But, by providing technical services, we interact a hundred times a day. This is why research institutes are so important: although they are unable to develop comprehensive technologies for commercialization on a large scale, they form an intermediate link between academic and industrial work by carrying out applied research." The institute charges a healthy fee for its services, and has attracted some 3 000 industrial clients.

The institute specializes in research on polymers, fibres, and environmental protection and does analytical testing for different industries. Its research and development in the field of plastics has placed it well ahead of other institutes. "No other institute in the world can claim to have developed as many plastic process technologies under one roof," says Nigam. "In this respect, the institute competes with major international organizations such as Dupont, ICI, Bayer, and General Electric." The technologies in the institute's portfolio include polyvinyl chloride (PVC), polystyrene, high-impact polystyrene, ABS plastics, polycarbonate, and polyacetals.

Another of the institute's recent projects was an upgrading of silk technology. After examining the level of development in silk production within the country, Nigam realized that the industry was starved of technological inputs. "Silk production is viewed in India as an art, rather than a technology. When you consider the stiff competition coming from Japan and China, who produce silk of a superior quality, the drawbacks to Indian silk are apparent. Yet this is a large sector in the country, and our economy stands to gain a lot from developing this technology."

With the idea of giving silk production a technological orientation, which would improve its quality and its export potential, Nigam and his colleagues set up a silk research centre in Bangalore. Joint ventures between India and other silk-producing countries are being pursued. Other projects include developing fire-resistant composites used for space shells and optimizing the process used to produce Kevlar, which is used in bullet-proof vests.

Recycling of various waste materials is another initiative of the institute. Nigam has always been interested in the potential of recycling. When he lived in England during his student years, he used to collect all his old newspapers and plastic cartons, with the idea of selling them. But nobody was willing to buy them. "Recycling is a relatively new concept in the West. In India, we have been recycling for years — every middle-class household sells its junk — old newspapers, bottles, tins, and so on. Most of the paper we use is recycled. To some extent our society has taught the recycling concept to others."

While Dr Nigam worked at J.K. Synthetics, he noticed that a neighbouring carbide plant, Shriram PVC, generated a huge amount of lime sludge that lay piled outside. The Shriram company approached the J.K. Synthetics research labs to develop a process to convert the sludge into cement, to be used at the Shriram cement factory. When Nigam joined the institute, he took on this project. "Using the waste generated from the carbide factory we were able to optimize the process of converting this into cement for the Shriram Cement company. This is the second or third plant of its kind in the world to use this technology." SRI's other recycling successes are the conversion of Teflon (PTFE) waste into lubricating grease — the first time that Teflon waste has been reused anywhere in the world.

Yet another successful recycling project converts rice-husk waste into precipitated silica. Rice husk used in boilers generates several million tonnes of ash, which is dumped everywhere and is becoming a major source of pollution. The conversion of this ash into precipitated silica, used in various products (rubbers, plastics, and toothpaste) is clearly an extremely beneficial process. SRI is second to the German company Degussa, in optimizing this process.

A major ongoing project, funded by IDRC, is the conversion of boiler fly-ash into cement. "The fly ash generated as a by-product of thermal boilers is dumped everywhere, causing widespread pollution. This can be converted to a useful product: cement. Today, we have managed to use 12 to 15 percent of fly ash in the raw mixture to make portland cement. The project is serving two important purposes: reducing the pollution caused by fly ash and generating useful bricks."

While proud of SRI's performance and its subsequent contribution to industrial development, Nigam is today concerned about the general lack of technological progress in the country. He has been working on a book, *Made in India*, that challenges the way Indian industries are run. Although he doesn't intend to publish the text right away, the process of writing it has helped relieve his frustration over the poor state of industrial development in the country.

His strong views about what constitutes development in a society often create storms in more conservative sections of the scientific community. According to him, adopting international standards at par with advanced countries or programs that do not have relevance in a particular society create social and economic problems and disrupt the process of development.

"What is the point of getting involved in issues that are still uncertain and have less relevance in poorer, developing countries like India, such as the search for CFC [chlorofluorocarbon] substitutes? We do not even have resources to provide clean drinking water in the best equipped cities like Delhi and Bombay, nor can we implement the Clean Air Act properly, or handle our local wastes, or maintain our rivers without external assistance. What is the justification, then, for worrying about CFCs? Unless the technology of substitutes is economical and available to us at nominal costs, and does not hurt our national and industrial interests, we must not accept the terms for phasing out CFCs, at our cost."

The ultimate benefactor of technology should be the people on the street, says Nigam. "The aim of technological processes is to generate products useful to the ordinary person. Relevant technology should improve the quality of life for men and women and their community. Adopting technologies that cater to a minority in the society will only slow down development," he says. "This is one reason the textile industry is not developing at the rate it should be. Just because Pierre Cardin and Christian Dior have arrived in India doesn't mean our textile industry is any better at catering to the needs of the ordinary man. High fashion garments are meant for a small minority of rich people in the country. What we need to do is apply the same emphasis presently being placed on exports, to textile development for the larger population."

Ritu Bhatia is a New Delhi-based journalist who writes on issues of environment, public health, and population for such leading publications as The Times of India *and* The Indian Express.

WASEY OMAR
(Pakistan)

Throughout much of his distinguished career as a mechanical engineer, Wasey Omar has concentrated his time and effort on inventing a better "dobby," a device used in textile machinery to produce patterned fabric. Omar's new low-cost dobby has the potential to revolutionize the textile industry in Asia and improve productivity and income levels of many family-run cottage industries in his native Pakistan, as well as in India and China. Omar wryly admits that his successful invention was largely due to his incomplete understanding of weaving: not knowing all about the process freed him up to seek more independent, unconventional solutions.

by Nabila Zar

BORN IN CHITTAGONG, EAST BENGAL IN 1927, WASEY Omar spent most of his childhood in a small town in Indian Punjab surrounded by books and an enriched learning environment. His maternal grandfather was a distinguished educator and his paternal grandfather was a scholar who served as a senior physician to the Maharajas of Jammu and Kashmir for two generations. He left behind a huge library containing over 100 000 books. It was here, roaming through the book stacks, that young Omar developed a taste for reading.

As a boy, Omar traveled widely and visited most of the historical places in Kashmir, Delhi, Agra, and Calcutta in the company of his lawyer father. "My most cherished memories as a young boy are of wandering in Elora Caves near Bombay with my father and hiking in the Kulu Range of the Himalayas with friends."

His first introduction to science was in the sixth grade, and he immediately developed a fascination for scientific experiments. He vividly remembers the hours of enjoyment studying science on his own and using his spending money to buy scientific gadgets and apparatus. Elementary kits of Meccano were sent to him by his grandfather in Calcutta. One special book, a gift from his father, was *Nine-in-One Magic Toys, For Every Modern Girl and Boy*. The book was made of perforated cardboard sheets from which one could build a "powerhouse" and other working models. "These early hobbies," he says today, "had a great influence on my later life and choice of work."

With the partition of India, his family migrated to Pakistan and settled in Sindh, where his father had bought about 200 hectares of land when the first dam (Sukkur Dam) and canals were built on the Indus River in the 1930s. Omar graduated from the Government College in Lahore with a degree in mathematics and later obtained a master's degree in physics. After graduation, he found a job in a textile mill.

Omar's decision to work in textiles was not accidental. He had been hoping for just such an opening. He had long believed that textiles held great potential for the future of Pakistan and that any new developments in this industry could improve the lives of millions of people and give Pakistan a competitive edge in world markets.

In India, Pakistan, and China the textile industry is extremely important: it not only provides enough clothing for the 2 billion local inhabitants, it earns much-needed foreign exchange. In Pakistan, textile products account for 60 percent of total exports. Most of the export-quality cotton fabric is produced by small, family-run cottage industries. The weavers still use ancient looms for the production of plain fabric. Small weaving enterprises (often family run) can earn 20 to 25 percent more by producing designed (geometric or floral) patterns rather than plain cloth.

The printed fabric is produced on the loom using a mechanical selection device called a "dobby." Currently, two types of dobbies are used: modern dobbies, which are efficient, high speed, and expensive; and older, less efficient, cheaper dobbies used throughout the developing world. It was always Omar's hope to develop a fast and efficient dobby that would still be relatively inexpensive and easy to make locally.

One day in July 1955, while reading a book on jacquards and dobbies, he had an idea. He would do what multinational firms had failed to do in more than 100 years — invent a new kind of dobby that would remove all of the flaws inherent in its mechanism. Without realizing the difficulties that lay ahead, he quickly borrowed 1 000 rupees from his father and started building a model dobby. The century-old technology being used by the textile industry the world over had to give way, he was convinced. He worked out in his mind a simpler, low-cost yet efficient machine that would replace the original one. This dream, he was to discover, would take a lifetime of hard work to realize.

His dobby research began in earnest, and the first patent was filed in the United Kingdom in 1956. That year was a difficult one in his personal life. Two of his strongest supporters, his grandmother and father, died in quick succession. He had been deeply attached to his grandmother, for it was she who had raised him following the death of his mother when he was a child. Shortly after the death of his father, the family was forced to leave a small but powerful religious society that they belonged to. This meant a complete break with the familiar past: society, friends, and beliefs. At that time, the only link he retained with the past was the dobby research that he had started a year before. Amid the personal pain, he concentrated all his energies on his research.

For a long time, Omar's main problem was convincing the administration and other relevant quarters, including foreign embassies, of the usefulness of his work to obtain research funds. Eventually, he obtained the cooperation of Colony Textile Mill Ltd, Multan. There, a talented young mechanic named Masud helped him to fabricate his early prototypes.

In 1963, Omar's work was recognized for the first time. He was awarded the first research prize in Pakistan by a committee headed by the Pakistan Council of Scientific and Industrial Research (PCSIR). Along with the award, he was offered a job at PCSIR, the only centre of its kind in the country. However, textile research was not part of PCSIR's work at that time, and Omar's project was put on the backburner.

Missing his dobby work, Omar felt an intense need to share his ideas with others and to acquire further knowledge and skill to complete his research. Eventually, a professor (Grosberg) from the University of Leeds was sufficiently impressed by Omar's linear dobby research to reserve him a seat for a PhD course in the field. But Omar did not have enough money to study in the United Kingdom. He says it was the only time he felt sorry for himself and his humble circumstances.

Finally, in 1970, as a member of PCSIR, he was selected for a diploma course in industrial engineering by the federal government of West Germany in Bonn. And, in 1976, the Government of Pakistan awarded him a grant of CA $30 000, followed by another grant in 1982 of 100 000 rupees,[1] for the construction of a weaving shed for the project.

In Omar's view, developing countries such as Pakistan find it increasingly difficult to come up with funds for research. They have to look to western countries for assistance. In his case, the assistance came from Canada's International Development Research Centre and the Manitoba Research Council. In 1987, IDRC started funding the development of a baulkless single-lift dobby, initially named the PAKCAN Dobby. Work is now underway in India to produce this machine commercially.

Omar's current project is the development of the double-lift dobby. Work on this project has already reached an advanced stage, and the first prototype of this machine is expected soon. It is anticipated that the earlier single-lift dobby together with the new double-lift version will fulfil a genuine need in the weaving industry of the South. Omar's work will also benefit

---

[1] Today, 1 Pakistani rupee (PKR) is equivalent to about 5 Canadian cents.

the cottage-powerloom sector of the subcontinent and of China. Of the estimated 2 billion workers in this field, about 70 percent will benefit from this invention.

Commenting on the pace of development in the field of science and technology in his country, Omar said: "In Pakistan there has been considerable development in the processing industries based on locally available raw material. These industries include textile, sugar, fertilizers, and cement. In other fields, especially engineering related to capital machinery and energy production, Pakistan has a long way to go.

"Textile production is gradually shifting from the North to the South, but the related capital machinery, especially the modern powerlooms and dobbies, have been made too complicated and too costly.

"Efforts in the public sector of Pakistan to manufacture textile machinery through imported technology have not been successful. China and India also still depend on older models of powerlooms and dobbies. My contribution in developing a local technology for low-cost high-performance dobbies for the region is a rare effort from the South."

Omar's view is that information sharing within the South and between the North and the South is critically important. The South by itself is not in a position to develop an idea from the laboratory level to the production stage. And political problems do not usually allow the sharing of information within the South. It is in this area that the North can play a very constructive role, he says.

His experience in taking research from the laboratory level to the production or semiproduction stage has mainly come from contact with the Manitoba Research Council. Important professional development opportunities, such as his visit to the Bombay Textile Research Association (BTRA), would not have been possible without IDRC's help, he says. It provided him with an opportunity to exchange views with researchers engaged in similar work, which added to his confidence about the usefulness of his own work.

Ironically, Omar credits his ingenuity in part to a lack of detailed knowledge about the weaving process. When he began his research in 1955, Omar did not fully appreciate the importance of such technical features as open-shed, double-lift, and baulk, which were features of the prevailing Hattersley system that had been the model for the previous 100 years.

With his own thought process "unbiased," he evolved independent solutions to the problems that had been faced and solved earlier. The new dobby developed by Omar and his research colleagues is fast and efficient, as well as being relatively inexpensive and easy to make locally. Its advantages over conventional dobbies in current use include: superior stability, perfect alignment, few components, vibration-free, lighter, and reduced energy consumption.

After 18 years of research, Wasey Omar has invented a simpler piece of equipment. It is not an improved version of the existing equipment, but, rather, it operates on a different principle that makes the whole mechanism much simpler — a mechanism that requires only two moving parts for each filament rather than ten. This new invention is much smaller and only one-tenth the cost of the existing imported dobbies.[2]

At 67 years of age, Omar is still obsessed with his research work. Winning the 1993 Rolex honourable mention award for inventing a baulkless double-lift dobby has given him new hopes for the success of his current work. Although retired for the past 7 years, he still follows meticulously his work routine. His home computer-aided design (CAD) equipment and his son, Khalid, are his only companions for most of the day, and sometimes even at nights.

---

[2] Currently, dobbies are expensive because they must be imported from West Germany, Japan, or Switzerland and paid for in foreign currency. They can cost ten times as much as a used loom, or more than US $10 000 per unit.

Given the size of the industry and the number of looms used, it is clear that there is a vast potential market for Omar's new model of the dobby. Consider the following: about one-third of the looms in the Third World use a dobby; 50 percent of these dobbies now in use will have to be replaced over the next 10 years. This brings the potential market for the Omar invention to 2.4 million. The largest markets include China and India, which each have more than 500 000 looms, followed in decreasing order by Pakistan, Brazil, Indonesia, Thailand, Egypt, and Turkey. There are still an estimated 1.7 million looms without dobbies. Cost effectiveness and profitability can be enhanced by adding dobbies to their spindles.

Omar and his wife, Farida, have one son and two daughters, all of whom have followed scientific curricula in local universities. Omar readily acknowledges how important the support of his family has been to him through the years. "It has been a long, difficult struggle at times, and I am blessed with a family that has stood by me through all sorts of setbacks. My wife, Farida, is a pillar of strength. Her optimism and faith in me have never wavered, even when things went wrong. As well, my late stepmother and mother-in-law have been a source of great moral encouragement and financial help in times of need. No one is luckier than me in this respect."

Nabila Zar is editor of Friday Review, *the main weekly magazine of Pakistan's prestigious English-language daily,* The Nation.

Gursaran Talwar
(India)

*A*fter 20 years of research, Gursaran has developed the world's first family-planning vaccine. It is a safe, long-lasting, reversible vaccine that will be of interest and benefit to the South and North alike. The scientific and research challenges have been considerable, and he also had to face the usual skepticism concerning Third World scientists. "For a scientist in a developing country to make an original contribution, he or she has to work five times harder."

by Usha Rai

TWENTY YEARS IS QUITE A LONG TIME TO DEVOTE TO A single research project, but this is how long it has taken Dr Gursaran Talwar to arrive at a remarkable achievement: a safe, long-lasting, reversible vaccine to prevent pregnancy in women.

Along the way, Talwar has had to battle scientific challenges and the disbelief of many foreign colleagues. "People felt it was a fantasy," he said of the reaction in the early 1970s to his idea of a birth-control vaccine. "Vaccines are traditionally made for diseases, pestilence, viruses, and bacteria — not birth control." He also faced the usual skepticism concerning Third World scientists. "For a scientist in a developing country to make an original contribution, he or she has to work five times harder," he said.

The idea of doing research for a contraceptive vaccine came to Talwar in the early 1970s when he was working as an executive council member of Banaras Hindu University in the state of Uttar Pradesh. Shuttling between Delhi and Banaras, he observed that most of the people were physically stunted from lack of proper nutrition. He learned that this was due to the small land-holdings in these communities. A full 63 percent of

India's farmers have less than 0.6 hectares of land. Because family size remains large (seven or eight children), land-holdings become fragmented as they are passed from father to sons. Small land-holdings cannot produce enough food to keep the families nourished. Forty percent of India's population lives below the poverty line.

Talwar's colleagues in the Department of Social and Preventive Medicine pointed out that, although it was not in the interest of Indians to have large families, there was not a wide choice of effective contraceptives. Vasectomy and tubectomy, offered to them through the official family planning programs, were terminal (nonreversible) methods. Intrauterine devices (IUDs) tended to cause excessive bleeding, which, in a population of women who already suffer from mass anemia, is not sustainable. Pills and condoms call for a high level of daily motivation.

So Talwar had an almost missionary zeal to work on a contraceptive that would have the following characteristics: not call for daily motivation; not have the risk of user failure; be reversible; and not disturb the menstrual cycle or cause bleeding. At the same time, the contraceptive should enable the woman to retain her privacy.

There is also a personal dimension to Talwar's motivation to work in this field. In India, where the majority of babies are born at home with the help of a birth assistant, tetanus is a major killer of young mothers. Talwar was born at home and his mother died 8 days after his birth. Although no one knows precisely what killed her, it could very well have been tetanus. The vaccine developed by Talwar is double-barreled in that it enables the generation of antibodies against human chorionic gonadotropin (hCG) and simultaneously raises antibodies against tetanus, giving women and newborns added protection.

Talwar began this research in 1975 as Professor of Biochemistry at the All India Institute of Medical Sciences, relying on financial support initially from the Family Planning Foundation of India and IDRC. His objectives called for a method radically different from previous attempts at birth control. Talwar's concept of the vaccine matched those objectives. It neither stops ovulation nor alters the menstrual cycle. Also, it does not require the motivation of taking a daily medication. Nor does it involve a doctor having to insert an IUD, which can cause irregular bleeding. Finally, it is reversible and allows women to retain their privacy.

The vaccine works by inducing the production in the body of antibodies to hCG, a hormone normally produced by the embryo to help prepare the uterus to accept implantation of the embryo. By increasing the production of antibodies that are able to inactivate hCG, this hormonal action is blocked and implantation of the embryo does not occur. Therefore, rather than trigger an abortion, the vaccine operates by helping to prevent the onset of pregnancy. In doing so, it simply heightens a natural process: about one-quarter of detectable conceptions fail because the embryo does not become implanted in the uterus. The vaccine induces the production of antibodies to hCG to a point where all embryos fail to become implanted.

Women who take the vaccine for the first time must have it administered once a month for 3 months, during which time they must use other forms of contraception. Dr Talwar is trying to develop a contraceptive for use during this period based on a natural product — the purified extract of the neem tree. Eventually, Talwar would like to refine the administration of the vaccine, so that a woman only has to visit a family-planning service once instead of three times. He is also working on formulations of the vaccine that will last for 6 months, 1 year, or 2 years.

Vaccinated women who later wish to become pregnant simply have to discontinue booster injections. The antibodies will disappear, hCG will no longer be neutralized, and an embryo will have a normal chance of implanting in the uterus.

According to Dr Don de Savigny, of IDRC's Health Sciences Division, the vaccine gives women a way to space births. "Ninety-nine percent of global maternal deaths occur in developing countries. This vaccine can help alleviate the problem of insufficient spacing as one of the reasons."

Recent clinical studies show that among 119 women immunized with the vaccine, only one pregnancy occurred over 1 224 menstrual cycles. Without the vaccine, 300 to 400 pregnancies would have been expected in such a group.

Talwar's work has been subjected to rigorous animal trials over a 10-year period. After having established the absence of side effects in animals and obtaining approval of the Drug Regulatory and Ethics Committee, safety trials were conducted in Brazil, Chile, Finland, India, and Sweden by The Population Council of New York. All of these studies confirmed that the vaccine was safe and that the effects were reversible. Subsequent tests, in three major Indian institutions, confirmed the ability of the vaccine to prevent pregnancy.

"We have passed an important milestone and that is to confirm that the vaccine works," says Talwar. Despite this success, however, it will be some time before the vaccine is ready for the public.[1] "My hope is that by the year 2000 it will be available for public use."

---

[1] Contraceptives require much more lengthy testing periods than those for medications against life-threatening diseases. One reason is that a contraceptive is meant for young, healthy people, who could be taking it over a period of up to 30 years.

The vaccine will have obvious benefits not just to countries of the South but to the entire world. "Many people want alternatives to current methods of contraception," says Talwar. "There is no dividing line between North and South. The vaccine does not block ovulation and it is usable at all stages of a woman's reproductive life."

Talwar insists on mentioning his gratitude to IDRC for its early support of his research. "Yes, it was a novel idea back then, greeted with skepticism by many in the beginning, but IDRC did not hesitate. It gave a grant to support the idea." Part of the reason may have been the reputation of the individual and his research institute.

Some of the best scientific research institutions in the world are in India, says Dr de Savigny. "Talwar's National Institute of Immunology is a world-class institution. Immunologists from all over the world come to work and study there. In fact, birth-control vaccines being developed in Australia and the United States are not as advanced as Talwar's vaccine."

As word of the revolutionary nature of the research has spread, money has poured in from The Rockefeller Foundation, the Department of Biotechnology of the Government of India, and others. But it was IDRC, Talwar insists, that bolstered support for the research when it was most needed. In India, support came from the late industrialist and visionary J.R.D. Tata, who personally met Talwar and ensured support through the Family Planning Foundation that he set up.

In researching for the hCG vaccine, there have been several spin-off vaccines and creams. Praneem, a purified extract of neem seeds, is currently being tested as a contraceptive vaccine on male monkeys. In tests thus far, despite sperm counts of almost zero, it appears that the male sex hormone, testosterone, is not decreased and libido remains unaffected. Unlike vasectomy, this is expected to be a fully reversible method. The research for a male contraceptive silences criticism that all new contraceptives are targeted exclusively at women.

Another unexpected bonus from the research is a polyherbal formulation that acts as a potent spermicide and against a variety of genital pathogens, including candida, gardenella, chlamydia, and herpes. Made from purified neem extract, reetha, and cinchona bark extract, this spermicide is on clinical trials in India, Brazil, China, the Dominican Republic, Egypt, and Nigeria. Studies in progress also indicate an inhibitory effect on the replication of HIV (human immunodeficiency virus), the virus responsible for AIDS.

"The hCG research has opened up a Pandora's box," says Talwar. Yet another vaccine, which controls the production of sex hormones, is on clinical trial in India and Austria. It has therapeutic qualities and is being used in the treatment of prostate cancer.

Although Talwar's interest lies in the control of fertility in humans and animals, he is also working on a vaccine for leprosy. It is currently in phase-three trials in hospitals in Delhi and in a large rural block in Uttar Pradesh.

Countries such as Mexico are testing the hCG vaccine for yet another purpose — its possible application in human lung-cancer patients for which no effective chemotherapy is currently available.

For a man well into his sixties, Dr Talwar has tremendous drive and energy, perhaps owing to his regular practice of yoga and a habit of climbing stairs rather than taking elevators. His scientific efforts have won him laurels from around the world. Among the many awards and titles, in 1991, he was decorated with the Officier de la Légion d'honneur by the President of

France and, in 1992, he was awarded the prestigious Padma Bhushan prize by the President of India.

Recognized and admired in India and by the world at large, Gursaran (Pran) Talwar is a truly remarkable humanitarian whose impressive life's work promises to help improve the lives and futures of millions of people the world over.

Usha Rai is the recipient of several journalism awards and is currently development editor for The Indian Express *in New Delhi.*

Vo-Tong Xuan
(Viet Nam)

Agronomist Dr Vo-Tong Xuan lead the transformation of post-war Viet Nam from a heavy importer of rice to the third-largest rice producer in the world. Dr Xuan is devoted to improving the standard of living for his fellow Vietnamese, especially its farmers. A university vice-rector and a member of the Vietnamese National Assembly, Dr Xuan holds many awards for his work. A modest man, he doesn't dwell unduly on past achievements: his eye is to the future and the challenges that still await.

by Eileen Conway

DR VO-TONG XUAN IS LIVING PROOF THAT ONE PERSON can make a substantial difference in the world. Born in 1940 to a poor family in An Giang in southern Viet Nam, Dr Xuan is now Vice-Rector of the University of Cantho and a member of the Vietnamese National Assembly. Perhaps most impressive of all, Dr Xuan is credited with leading the transformation of post-war Viet Nam from a rice importer to the third-largest rice exporter in the world, all within one decade.

To fully understand this genial, modest, self-possessed man, you must know two things about him: one, he has a deep love for his country; two, he is a tireless champion of the Vietnamese farmer. Virtually everything he has achieved or ever tried to achieve — and certainly most of the personal sacrifices that he and his wife and children have made over the years — have all sprung from these two passions.

"My personal goal in life is to serve my country and to work on behalf of the Vietnamese farmer," he says. He is passionately dedicated to the elimination of rural poverty throughout Viet Nam and to helping his country rebuild and prosper.

To appreciate the magnitude of the achievement in rice production, consider the hurdles that were involved. For the plan to succeed, it required convincing the Marxist government to put aside the collective system of agriculture in favour of land tenure to individual farmers; it involved developing in the fields better technologies such as high-yield rice varieties; it required training and inspiring a large cadre of agricultural extension workers; and, perhaps most challenging of all, it involved educating and motivating millions of peasant farmers in Viet Nam to modify their traditional way of farming and accept new technologies and techniques generated by agricultural research.

The push for increased rice production began in the late 1970s at a difficult time in Viet Nam's history when the country lay in a grim, war-ravaged state of deprivation and uncertainty. Politicians and bureaucrats in the capital and in the provinces did not necessarily think in a concrete or systematic way about how to improve rice production. In fact, some were openly suspicious of new ways to improve production. Yet Dr Xuan is exceptionally single-minded. His quiet persistence and persuasive powers can never be underestimated. If ever there was a man with a mission, it is he. And he succeeded against the odds.

Yet, how is it that this man — son of a poor clerk and raised in the city — should have chosen the life of agricultural research and advocacy on behalf of the Vietnamese farmer, when he himself is not even remotely from a farming background? "I do not come from a farm, it's true," he admits. "My family was poor, my father was a clerk, and we moved several times when I was a child, but always we lived in towns or cities. During high school exams, however, I used to escape the noise of the city and go for study breaks to my uncle's farm in the country. I remember being utterly amazed at how hard he worked, the long, long hours of work and toil, and yet how little financial gain he received. He and all his neighbours were the same: they all lived in extreme poverty."

When he finished high school, he wanted to pursue university studies and, in fact, engineering was his first choice. However, scholarships in engineering were available only to the richer students. Poorer students, if accepted, were given scholarships to study agriculture.

There are those exceptional individuals whose intelligence, energy, practical approach, and emotional and mental agility ensure that they will succeed in whatever field of endeavour they choose to pursue, and this is true of Dr Xuan. From an early age, Dr Xuan has always been attuned to opportunities and has never been afraid of the hard work that success almost invariably entails.

"My father earned almost nothing in his job and so, as a family, we all had to pitch in and work hard to survive. I now have an appreciation for how precious hard work and labour is. As a boy, I usually had one or two part-time jobs selling newspapers, guarding cars, whatever I could get, and of course also keeping up with my schoolwork. I feel lucky I did not come from a rich family, as I can appreciate the importance of work and I sympathize with other people who labour."

Having chosen agriculture as a career, he set out to become a top-notch agronomist. He studied agricultural chemistry at the University of the Philippines from 1969 to 1971, specializing in sugar technology. A number of his friends worked at the Ministry of Agriculture in Viet Nam and when they visited him in the Philippines, they talked about how the future of agriculture in Viet Nam would be in the Mekong Delta and that rice production would be key. "I realized that if I came back to Viet Nam with my sugar-technology knowledge, it would not be useful."

So he approached the International Rice Research Institute (IRRI) in Los Baños and requested a position as an unsalaried apprentice: he simply wanted to learn all he could about rice and then return to Viet Nam and apply that knowledge. During this time he was also earning money as a translator, and one particular assignment proved to be extremely valuable to his professional development: he was hired to translate all the materials for a course on the training of trainers for the World Health Organization's (WHO) malaria-eradication specialists.

"By the time I finished, I knew the course materials better than the official trainees, and I felt that this training approach could be adapted and used in rice-production training." IRRI eventually hired him to teach training, and he developed a book called *Training Manual for Rice Production*, which IRRI published in eight languages and which is still in use.

The personal sacrifices he has made to stay and work in Viet Nam have been many, but there have been two times in his adult life when the "moment of decision" was quite dramatic. "There are two occasions that stand out. The first was in 1971 in the Philippines when I realized that I had sufficient experience with rice and I should use it in the Mekong Delta. All this time I was thinking: with this kind of knowledge, if I do not share and multiply it, what will happen to Viet Nam in the future? The University of Cantho contacted me at IRRI and asked if I would join the university. The first thing I had to do was to convince my wife that we should return home to Viet Nam. This was not an easy decision because I had a good job and, although we were not wealthy, I was able to avoid the draft and the war. But in Asia, you know, we still believe in fate, in destiny. We must try first, and when some plan or wish does not work in the way we want, then maybe it is destiny or God speaking to us."

So his wife finally agreed and they moved with their two children back to Viet Nam on 9 June 1971. He joined the university and 2 months later, was drafted into the army. He went through 9 weeks of basic training until, through the intervention of the university president, he was granted a deferment and was able to return to his work.

The second time he faced a serious choice regarding his future in Viet Nam occurred in Japan in 1975. While teaching in Viet Nam and doing research on the Mekong Delta, he went to Japan for 6 months to complete work on his doctorate in agriculture. By February of that year, everyone knew that the end of the war was imminent. In the Japanese newspapers and on television, the Viet Cong had suddenly become the "liberating forces" for the South. "I seriously wondered whether this was a good time to return to Viet Nam, knowing the chaos, uncertainty, and danger that would be there.

"Yet during my time in Japan I had met many successful farmers, and I was so inspired to see farmers living happy lives. They had all kinds of science and technology to help them. I saw the children of Japanese farmers with plenty of toys and books and education, and the Japanese people generally have a very nice lifestyle. I thought constantly of my own people, my own two children and my sister's children, and all my neighbours. They too deserve nice things, I said to myself. And what of the Vietnamese farmer? Who is going to help him? It won't be the Russians or the Americans. No, it is up to us, the Vietnamese, to help one another. Our future is up to us alone. These were my thoughts at that time.

"So I returned on 2 April 1975 at a time when most of the traffic was going the opposite way, out of Viet Nam. When I got home the war had ended and some professors had already left. I and my fellow colleagues stayed behind and guarded the university from looting. The looting was really terrible at that time, people would just loot everything that was abandoned."

The communists took over the university and other institutions in the country. Many intellectuals and specialists fled Viet Nam feeling left out of the new system and believing that they could not continue their work without interference. Dr Xuan's experience was somewhat different, and he attributes it to luck and to his own style of working with people.

"First of all, the communist rector at our university was someone we could work with. He called a meeting of the university staff soon after he arrived and told us frankly that he had grade seven education and did not know anything about research. 'I don't know much about science — that is your area of knowledge — but I do know politics,' he told us. 'I have been fighting in the revolutionary force for 30 years and I know government and the political system, so let's work together. I have to make decisions on technology and science, so you give me your recommendations and I will pass these on to my political bosses.' "

Second, personality was a factor. "Possibly because I am not an arrogant person," Dr Xuan allows, "the communist leader of my university and I got along well, as he was also that way and so we understood each other very well. So that, briefly, is why my university was able to make a substantial contribution to the development of agriculture in the south and from there expanded to the north."

One of the keys to Dr Xuan's success has been his effective use of training. He knows that training is critical to ensuring that farmers and others involved in agriculture benefit from technological advances. When asked what has proven most effective, he says, without hesitation: "television."

He used a regular television show as a means of disseminating information about rice farming and related agricultural topics. With a camera crew, he filmed in various locations, always careful to include different local farmers in each episode to make it authentic and of interest. The show made him widely recognized in Viet Nam and he is sometimes called "Doctor Farmer" for the way he diagnoses problems and prescribes remedies for the problems that rice farmers bring to him.

"Television has been wonderful as a medium for education. The period 1978 to 1981 was crucial to our plan to increase rice production. We used television to spread the word about the new technology in high-yielding rice cultivation among farmers and agricultural extension workers and even government offices in the province, district, and villages. Television is available all over the southern part of Viet Nam. Even poor farmers can go in the evening over to the house of a neighbour with a television.

"Television is better than radio because the farmers can see for themselves," he says. "We planned the entire series and then did each show in logical sequence. Showing how the new rice is different from the old rice. It's always best with farmers to lead them from what they know to what they don't know. To lead them to what we want them to know in a way that does not surprise or intimidate them, but instead puts them at their ease."

Dr Xuan is currently involved with a project funded by IDRC and the Vietnam Farming Systems Network, which was begun in 1991 and is aimed at training people in farming systems research and extension methods. It also will develop appropriate agricultural systems that are economically and environmentally suitable. The project will improve farm and rural family incomes, nutrition, and welfare. Nearly 100 farming systems specialists have been trained so far, and they, in turn, are training other agriculture extension workers, ministry employees, and farmers. The project has developed various environmentally sound, economically sustainable farming systems such as sloping land agroforestry systems in the hilly and mountainous regions, and rice–fish or rice–shrimp systems in the freshwater and saline-water regions.

In September 1993, Dr Xuan was presented with the Ramon Magsaysay Award for Government Service in a ceremony in Manila. The Magsaysay Award is one of the most prestigious honours in Asia.

His wife of 32 years, Ngoc Le, has been devoted and unstinting in her support of her husband. His wife and three children are extremely important to Dr Xuan; family is everything to him. His own parents were very religious and he grew up in a close family. Today, in spite of an extremely busy schedule, he finds time for others and is described as generous and caring by friends and colleagues.

As to the future, what does he foresee for Viet Nam in the coming years? He points out that the area of policy is critical to the advancement of his country. "You can have the best technology in the world, but if the government policy is not conducive then the best products and programs will fail.

"Since 1977, we had been trying new varieties resistant to insects and to the brown planthopper and explaining how to use these varieties with proper fertilization, water management, and pest control. But all these could not be applied until the government removed the communist-style cooperative system. Imposing the cooperative system was just like tying the hands of the farmer." "Decollectivation" began in 1981, and it was then that the benefits of technology could be seen.

In the next 5 years, he foresees the need for changes in technology and policy. "On the technology side, we need to develop even better rice varieties that can produce yields of at least 20 percent more, and, at the same time, these varieties must offer good eating qualities so that people are prepared to buy the rice. We must develop more efficient ways of pest control so that we can be sure of a clean environment. Not just pest control but fertilization control, how to use water economically because water will continue to be a limited resource."

Dr Xuan hopes to solve the problem of postharvest losses, which now run at about 15 percent. This translates into a loss of 3 million tonnes or US $300 million every year.

Commercialization of appropriate technology is another challenge. "We want to find ways to manufacture locally the inventions by Vietnamese researchers — farming equipment is just one example — and ensure that this technology is available locally at a price that farmers and others can afford.

"On the policy side, the politicians must design better policy that offers greater incentives to the farmer. Because I am a member of the national assembly, I always try to push to create a political climate that is conducive to better agriculture. We need to address the serious growing gap between rich and poor farmers. We are seeing now that the rich farmers are getting richer, and the poor are falling behind and staying poor. We see that monoculture rice farmers remain the poorest in the farming communities, even if the agriculture policy is favourable. By contrast, farmers who diversify their crops using various farming systems are better off financially."

Lack of credit is hindering farmers, especially in the south. Without access to money for insecticides, fertilizers, seeds, and farm improvements, the poorer farmers are condemned to stagnate.

"So these will be my areas of concentration during the next 5 years, helping the poor farmer in the less-privileged areas in the lowlands, in the coastal areas, and in the highlands. Viet Nam is on the path to prosperity, although the advance is still slow. It is important to acknowledge all the political, economic, and social difficulties we have overcome. I am proud to have been part of that."

Eileen Conway, an Ottawa-based writer, was formerly editor-in-chief of IDRC Reports *magazine.*

ZHU ZHAOHUA
(China)

Son of a forest ranger, Zhu Zhaohua grew up amid bamboo and fir forests in Zhejiang Province, and it was here that his abiding love of nature blossomed. He went on to become a world-renowned forestry ecologist whose important research on the Paulownia tree and in agroforestry has helped immeasurably the ecology and agricultural output of his native China, and earned him international recognition in his field.

by Zhang Dan

CHINESE FOREST ECOLOGIST ZHU ZHAOHUA HAS HAD AN impressive career, although political events in his country have at times created substantial obstacles. The road to success for this world-renowned researcher has been marked with setbacks, but his persistent love of work has proved an essential driving force in his remarkable life.

It began in 1962, when he received a degree in botanical ecology from Lanzhou University in the northwestern province of Gansu and started work in China's central mountains researching secondary forestry. Four years later, his work was halted by the cultural revolution: he was sent to a village in the southern countryside to grow wheat, raise pigs, and cook for more than 100 people. "I was kept away from my studies for 6 years," he remembers with regret.

In 1972, Zhu finally returned to Beijing and the Chinese Academy of Forestry (CAF), but he couldn't resume his work immediately. He was assigned to dig air-raid shelters in preparation for the imminent invasion by the so-called "foreign capitalist devils." The invasion never happened, and 6 months later Zhu's life changed for the better. Officials from the Chinese Ministry of Forestry returned from an international congress with a request to supply Argentina with six kinds of *Paulownia* seeds. Two of them, *Paulownia elongata* and *Paulownia glabrata*, were then strangers to Chinese scientists, although the trees were thought to be indigenous to China. The Assistant Director of the Research Institute of Forestry of the CAF asked Zhu to do a search for the two kinds of trees.

"I knew very little about *Paulownia* at the time, and none of the experts I consulted knew of the two species," Zhu says. Finally, he happened to find descriptions of the trees in a back issue of a journal from Taiwan. Armed with that knowledge, he set off for Shandong and Henan provinces, in east and central China, in an effort to fulfil the Argentinean request.

And this is how Zhu returned to the research that had taken up so much of his professional life before the cultural revolution. "After so many years away from my studies, I was overjoyed to be assigned this task," he says. "I found the seeds I was looking for in Shandong, but I also found much more."

While familiarizing himself with *Paulownia*, Zhu recalled that during the difficult years in the early 1960s, a local official named Jiao Yulu in poverty-stricken Lankao County of Henan Province had encouraged people to plant the tree as protection against sandstorms, alkaline soil, and land erosion. "But I didn't know then it would be such a boon to farming," he says.

As he toured Shandong and Henan studying *Paulownia*, Zhu came to look upon it as a "wonder tree." It grows at a surprisingly fast speed, and, when planted alongside crops such as wheat, corn, and cotton, it enhances yield rates. What's more, the tree provides farmers with valuable timber; its twigs and branches make good firewood, and its broad leaves can be used as fodder for animals or as organic fertilizer.

Zhu became more and more interested in the tree's many uses. When he returned to Beijing with the seeds he had been sent to find, he submitted a report. He was encouraged to follow up on his investigations. "That was when I decided I would make *Paulownia* my life's work," he says.

From 1972 to 1977, Zhu became a Chinese "Johnny Appleseed" (only, in his case, it involved *Paulownia* seeds).

Carrying his heavy sample bag, Zhu trekked alone through more than 200 counties in twenty-two Chinese provinces, becoming more and more knowledgable about the distribution and various species of the tree throughout the country. It was a most difficult time for the scientist. He had to brave some very dangerous and remote mountain regions. But worst of all, those caught up in the hysteria of cultural revolution suspiciously regarded all research as opposition to the revolution. Fortunately for Zhu, his superiors encouraged and protected him.

"I knew his work was important, and I encouraged him to press on with it. Eventually all his research paid off," says Wu Zhonglun, then his boss and now one of the most famous forestry experts in China. Because Zhu had majored in botany, Wu advised him to train himself in agroforestry and agriculture so that he could research *Paulownia*'s many applications. Wu told his protégé that the key to success was breadth of knowledge. Zhu's knowledge proved both broad and deep. He gained a clear picture of China's *Paulownia* distribution and the optimum conditions for its growth. He also discovered three new species of the tree, raising the total in China to nine.

In 1975, Zhu began to promote the planting of *Paulownia* throughout the country. He first published part of his research in that year, and his findings met with considerable favourable response. The next year, the cultural revolution was over, and Zhu was able to do his work openly. He even got an annual stipend of 9 000 yuan (then equal to US $3 000) from the CAF, so he was able to propagate the tree by motivating farmers to participate in his field experiments.

In retrospect, Zhu says, "I don't think my biggest contributions are my scientific discoveries. True, I've discovered three new species, produced a number of clones, developed the formula for *Paulownia*–crop intercropping, and improved planting methods. Still, I think my major contribution has been to persuade officials and farmers to join in the transformation of the local environment by intercropping *Paulownia*."

Zhu and his colleagues traveled from village to village, convincing farmers of the tree's great value. They taught farmers how and where the tree should be planted. They even wrote plays with plots that centred on planting *Paulownia* to make their points in a more impressive and amusing way. "We've done a lot of work, and much of it has been successful," says Lu Xinyu, Zhu's close assistant and long-time friend.

Zhu and his team held seminars to train technicians in more than 350 counties. He met with more than 300 county governors at three different national forestry conferences. The field stations connected with his projects have received more than 30 000 visitors. "These people have all helped us to propagate our program."

China's elder statesman, Deng Xiaoping, paid a special visit to Yanzhou County, which was one of the experimental regions in Shandong Province. He had heard of the tree's many uses and wanted to see a stand of them for himself. State funding helped build six experimental stations, one for each of China's major climate zones.

By 1978, 1.3 million hectares of farmland had been intercropped with *Paulownia* in China (from 20 000 hectares in 1972), mainly on the central and eastern plains. Zhu estimates that more than 15 million farmers have benefited from the reforestation projects. The *Paulownia* coverage has since been maintained at the 1978 level on the plains.

In 1985, Zhu's achievements won him a measure of international fame. He was given the Man of the Trees Award from the Richard St. Barbe Baker Foundation in Canada, an organization established in honour of the late renowned ecologist who inspired and led the reforestation movement. This award is now given every year to an individual or organization that has made an outstanding contribution to forestry. Zhu was its first recipient.

As a matter of fact, Zhu was already acquainted with Mr Baker. They had met in 1982 in Beijing. The elderly ecologist was on a global tour, promoting environmental awareness. He visited Zhu's academy and personally planted a *Metasequoia* tree in front of the office building where Zhu now works. "I remember him as an energetic and happy old man with silver hair, surrounded by a crowd of children. I never dreamed that one day he would have an international award named after him and that I would be honoured in his name," Zhu says.

In 1982, IDRC began to finance CAF's research on *Paulownia*, bamboo, rattan, and firewood, enabling its research teams to obtain specialized training and select the best species for reforestation projects. There were experiments dealing with the intercropping of different species of *Paulownia* with food crops as well as investigations into the effects of trees on the microclimate, environmental ecology, and social economy.

From 1983 to 1991, the *Paulownia* research team produced seven clones from which 25 million root cuttings have been distributed among the nation's farmers. The cloned trees, whose average growing rate is 25 to 30 percent higher than ordinary species, add approximately 400 million yuan to the annual income of China's farmers.

From 1988 to 1990, IDRC provided another CA $380 000 in research funding. Zhu is most grateful for IDRC's support. "Funding support from Canada has been invaluable, and it inspires us to make every effort to do our best research. Our ultimate reward, and the thing that makes the investment worthwhile, is the help we can provide to the farmers," he says.

In 1986, after a decade and a half of research on *Paulownia*, Zhu began to place his research in a broader perspective. "I began to focus my attention on agroforestry, also known as farm forestry," he recalls. Agroforestry is more than simply planting trees in fields. Apart from technical research, farm forestry emphasizes the "social–economic approach," as Zhu describes it.

In 1990, Zhu Zhaohua's group embarked on one of the most comprehensive agroforestry projects in China. It conducted fifteen subsidiary projects, and one of the major programs is still intercropping agricultural crops with *Paulownia*.

A typical example of a successful agroforestry project is Liuminying Village south of Beijing. Zhu and some of his colleagues first visited Liuminying in 1990 to assess the village's achievements in agroforestry because it had been recognized as a model ecological community by the United Nations some 3 years earlier. The results of Zhu's study were not particularly encouraging. To justify its reputation as an ecologically advanced community, Liuminying would have to achieve a substantial increase in its meager tree coverage of 6.1 percent by planting trees in and around fields, while increasing its crop yields. That was a tall order.

However, Zhu and his colleagues proved more than equal to the task. Acting on the results of their findings, they provided the villagers with *Paulownia* and willow saplings, and they taught them planting techniques. In the beginning it seemed too much to ask of the village, which had only 900 inhabitants and 117 hectares of cultivated land; nevertheless, in 1991, the villagers spent the equivalent of US $20 000 and gave up more than 11 percent of their precious land for the stands of *Paulownia* trees. "At the time even I doubted the wisdom of the sacrifices we were making," recalls Zhang Kuicheng, the village head, always an enthusiastic advocate of Zhu's approach.

By the second year of the project, the results were already more than encouraging. The newly planted trees and grass began to mature in the fields and around the farmers' houses. By 1993, with the planting of a 10-hectare orchard, trees covered nearly 20 percent of the village lands. "That was the best ratio in all of China's plains areas," says Zhu. "Any more forestation would have negatively affected crop yields."

Even with the decrease in arable lands, by 1993, Liuminying had increased its harvest by 38 percent over the

1990 output. "That is partly because we applied better cultivation methods, but I believe the trees were by far the most important reason for the increase," says Zhang. "Without Mr Zhu's help, this would have been impossible."

Zhu is project coordinator of an agroforestry project in the subtropical mountainous regions in southern China, concentrating on finding new ways to grow and use bamboo. The researchers there breed new strains of bamboo, grow mushrooms in bamboo groves, process bamboo shoots and mushrooms, and explore ways to keep these crops fresh. They conduct investigations into the nutritional value and potential economic returns of the products they develop. As well, they have set up experimental planting stations and publicized the results of the research.

In 1991, Zhu was named Director of the International Farm Forestry Training Center, a branch of CAF, providing short-term training for agroforestry workers from China and abroad. In the past 3 years, about 130 scientists from over twenty countries have participated in five international training courses sponsored by the centre.

The farm forestry project, which has occupied so much of Zhu's time and energy over the past years, was scheduled to end in 1994. Almost 900 000 hectares of land have now been planted with *Paulownia*, bamboo, Chinese fir, and other trees. The project has increased annual rural earnings by 170 million yuan (US $19.5 million).

"China is perhaps doing more agroforestry work than any other country in the world," Zhu says. "A gigantic shelter belt running through northwest, north, and northeast China, is being planted to combat desertification. China's agroforestry is now technologically advanced, but in the past we have not paid much attention to the social aspects of agroforestry research. We need to place more emphasis on this in the future." By "social aspects" Zhu means the relationship between forestation projects and government policies, local economic conditions, and demography.

Zhu has more ambitious projects in mind. He hopes to establish cooperation between Chinese and Indian forestry research institutes. "These are the two most populous nations in the world, and we should join forces to develop new approaches to agricultural forestry," Zhu says. "It would clearly be of great benefit to both countries and to the rest of the world."

Over the past three decades, Zhu has gone from digging air-raid shelters to receiving international acclaim. He has made remarkable achievements in his field, enormously increasing productivity and wealth in China, while helping to preserve the environment. Yet, if you passed him on the street, you would never guess he had accomplished great things. He is a rather small, unprepossessing 56-year-old man with grey hair and a dark suit.

Zhu's daily life is outwardly uneventful. After work he goes home to a small, simply furnished, one-bedroom apartment. After supper he and his wife watch the seven-o'clock news on television, then Zhu retires to the bedroom to spend some time with his old friends — his radios.

Zhu has five full-band world radio receivers. Whenever he travels he always takes one of them with him. Listening to the radio is his one hobby. "Radio is the greatest human invention," he says. "It is always there, whether you are at work, at play, or at home. It can keep you company 24 hours a day, and it never gets tired. The radio is my hotline to the outside world."

A somewhat reticent man, Zhu nevertheless becomes animated when he talks about his work: his weathered faced breaks into a smile, and he gestures emphatically to make his points. Over the years his communication skills have served him well. "My ability to give an entertaining and convincing lecture has helped me gain the support of farmers around the country," he says, flashing one of his winning smiles.

Zhu's fondness for nature is practically a genetic inheritance. His father was a forest ranger who managed more than 20 hectares of bamboo in Ling'an County of Zhejiang Province in China's southeast. "We lived in the mountains, and our home was surrounded by a dense bamboo forest," he recalls. "We lived on bamboo." In the winter, his family went into the hills to dig bamboo shoots; they sold the shoots to earn a living. He lived in that house in Ling'an until he was 18. He enrolled in Lanzhou University in 1957.

Zhu's enthusiasm is contagious, and he hopes that the younger generation will come to share it. To make that happen, he has already made some very active "retirement" plans. "When I retire from my job, I am going to travel through China's rural areas, village by village, teaching the children how important trees and forests are to us. I want them to love nature as much as I do."

In other words, Zhu hopes to follow in Richard Baker's footsteps. This is exactly what the eminent global ecologist did in his later years — travel from country to country, from village to village, preaching ecological awareness. This is what Baker was doing when he planted that tree that still shades Zhu's office in Beijing. The task is both arduous and crucial, given the many dangers now threatening China's fragile environment. "I want to follow Mr Baker's worthy example and contribute to the greening of our Earth," Zhu says. "I want to be a man of trees until the day I die."

Zhang Dan is a staff writer with China Features, *a news organization providing English and Chinese feature stories for overseas publications.*

Portraits of Development Research

▶ Zhu Zhaohua considers his major achievement to be his success in persuading farmers and officials to intercrop *Paulownia* trees on farmland, thereby transforming local environments.
See page 92

For Palmira Ventosilla, the biggest challenges in developing her method of biological control of mosquito larvae were outside the laboratory — convincing communities to apply her method.
See page 138 ▼

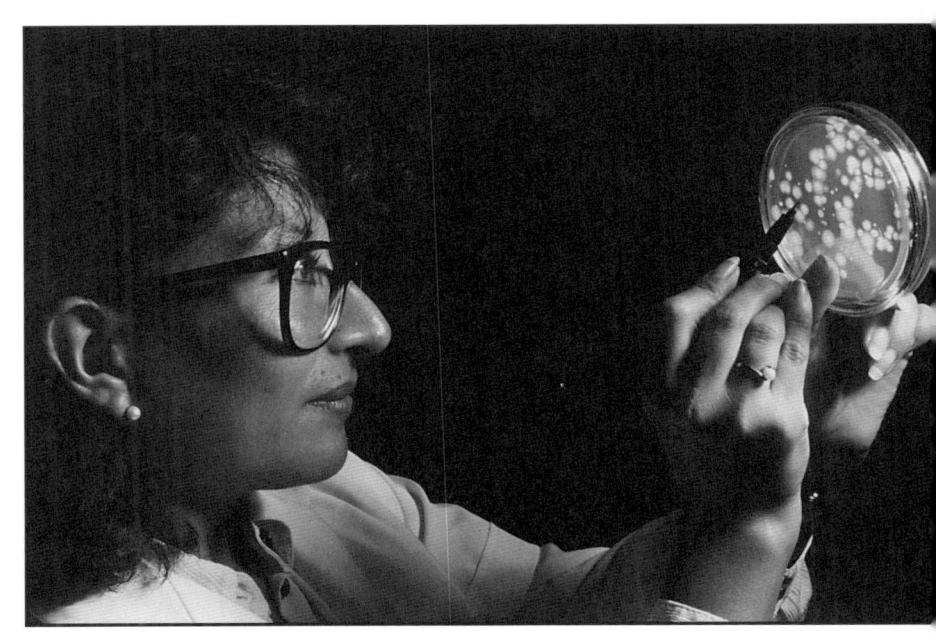

▲ Over the course of his research on essential oils, Guy Collin realized that technical expertise must be accompanied by sound knowledge of socioeconomic conditions in communities. *See page 144*

Pierre Sané possesses the strength of spirit essential to confronting terrible human rights abuses around the world.
See page 14
◄

For Pilar Cereceda, it is vital that research be applied to helping people solve their problems, rather than languish unused in professor's offices.
See page 114 ▶

Rural sociologist Gelia Castillo has been influential both as a researcher — on topics such as participatory development — and as a board member of international scientific organizations.
See page 36 ▼

▲ Among Eusèbe Alihonou's primary activities is building capacity in health, research, and program delivery from his base in Pahou, Benin. *See page 4*

▲ In collaboration with Chinese scientists, Charles Schafer (right) and John Norton Smith have contributed to strengthening China's capacity in marine research for environmentally safe harbours. *See page 152*

Joyce Robinson's greatest satisfaction comes from knowing she has made significant contributions to Jamaica's development.
See page 126
▶

◀ Gursaran Talwar's development of a safe, reversible contraceptive vaccine gives women a new choice in reproductive control.
See page 74

▲   Vo-Tong Xuan, agronomist and politician, is dedicated to improving conditions for farmers in Viet Nam and eliminating rural poverty.
See page 82

▼   During his lifetime, the late Jai Krishna Nigam exemplified the positive role of scientists in building indigenous capacity for technology development. *See page 56*

▲ After many years of research, Wasey Omar's invention of an efficient, low-cost dobby will benefit millions of workers in the weaving industries of Asia. *See page 66*

▼ African women are among the potential beneficiaries of Patricia Stamp's research, which has produced valuable insight on the interactions of gender, indigenous knowledge, technology, and power. *See page 172*

▲ Pilar Cereceda believes there are many more great ideas — such as the fog collector — within South American universities that could help disadvantaged communities. *See page 114*

▲ For Eusèbe Alihonou, researchers in the South must conduct what he calls "action research" aimed at removing obstructions to improvements in living conditions.
See page 4

▶
Bti (*Bacillus thuringiensis* var. *israelensis* serotype H-14) incubated at low cost inside coconuts is released into ponds where it kills mosquito larvae and disrupts mosquito breeding.
See page 138

▲ Joyce Robinson has played key roles in youth training, broadcasting, literacy, and library services in Jamaica.
See page 126

Mountain rivers were just one of many challenges to be surmounted by Hans Schreier and a Nepali research team in the search for sustainable farming technologies. *See page 162* ▼

▲   Industries such as tea production stand to benefit from Hari Gunasingham's innovations in more efficient process control technologies for agriculture in the South. *See page 46*

Lala Steyn puts into practice the idea of researchers working as activists to help empower local people in their struggles. *See page 24*   ▼

Pilar Cereceda
(Chile)

Her research using fog-catching nets to bring fresh water to isolated villages in her native Chile has given Pilar Cereceda a unique opportunity to have a positive impact on the lives of others. Where possible, she says, research should be taken out and used to improve people's lives. She derives deep satisfaction from her teaching and research, and her happiest moments are spent exploring the exquisite remote beauty of the Chilean landscape.

by Maria de Luigi

RETURNING TO THE TINY SEASIDE VILLAGE OF Chungungo (population 330) in northern Chile is quite often an emotional experience for Pilar Cereceda, researcher and geography professor at the University of Chile in Santiago.

Fourteen years ago, when Cereceda first arrived to begin her research project, Chungungo was just one of hundreds of villages in the region that had no local source of fresh water. The village sits in Chile's north coastal desert, just south of the Atacama, the most arid desert in the world. The inhabitants used to have water trucked in from 40 kilometres away, at a cost of US $8 per 1 000 litres. The average family had only 14 litres a day and, during drier periods, just 3 litres (in comparison, the average Canadian household consumes 300 litres daily per person).

Now, 14 years later, thanks to the introduction of an innovative fog-catchment system, the village has a fully functioning local water-supply system. The change is remarkable. Now that fresh water is more plentiful, local gardens burst with lettuce, tomatoes, beans, corn, even flowers. "When I visit, people stop me just to show me the shower in their homes!" says Cereceda.

The "miracle" of clean fresh water for the residents of Chungungo came about through the introduction of large fog collectors: "a kind of volleyball net, which captures the fog [called *camanchaca*], typical of northern Chile," explains Cereceda who, together with Dr Robert Schemenauer of Environment Canada, has directed and advised on the installation of these nets in other sites in Chile, Ecuador, Peru, and the Arabian Desert.

The process involves the installation of polypropylene mesh nets, 12 metres long and 4 metres high, situated high in the mountains above the village. Fog, which is a regular phenomenon in the area, passes through the mesh and leaves behind droplets that trickle down to a trough that carries the water to a storage tank in the village.

The 75 fog collectors built by the Chilean Forestry Service (CONAF) near Chungungo feature 3 600 square metres of mesh that, over the past 2 years, have captured an average of 10 000 litres of water daily. Chungungo has gone from being a village barely able to scratch out an existence to a prosperous community that even attracts holiday visitors. During the high season, the population of Chungungo grows by over 500, with attendant economic benefits to the local community. New houses are springing up.

CONAF equipped 1 hectare with drip-irrigation systems and handed out seeds, plants, and tools to begin farming in the area. "The change in the population's approach to agriculture has been slow, mainly because for many years the migrant fishermen who live here traveled constantly all over the Chilean coastline in search of good fishing. But now, some families have started to obtain successful results from their gardens. Some women have also received help on how to clean and sell fish, thus increasing their income considerably.

"I still remember the day the village of Chungungo inaugurated the water system. This is something they never, ever thought would come to their village," recalls Cereceda. "The inhabitants hired a translator and put up an English sign at the village entrance saying Thank You Canada."

There has been an extraordinary change of attitude in the people. "They realize that previously they had lived totally abandoned and that now they have the right to demand help from the municipal and regional authorities. They have confidence and real expectations. After receiving water and now electricity from the National Power Network System, people are now about to install a television-signal repeater antenna, something they never dreamed of before!"

Are there many other arid places in the world that could benefit from this same system? "Yes, definitely. The most important requirement, obviously, is that there be a mountain near the coast and clouds, with the appropriate characteristics, that can be intercepted by that mountain. If the cloud is at the right altitude and the prevailing winds favourable, then a layer of fog will skim the ground.

"Imagine, for thousands of years, the inhabitants of deserts have watched clouds pass overhead, while practically dying of thirst. What we have achieved, at sites with the adequate topography and space available for installing the fog collectors, is a successful system for taking droplets captured by the mesh and channeling them together where they become the miracle of potable water that flows forth from a tap in each home. Although many places appear to meet the necessary requirements, it is always essential to carry out a professional evaluation in each case to determine the most suitable terrain."

To this end, Cereceda investigates clouds, the wind, and water flows on site with her rain gauges, anemometers, and fog collectors. "What we did in Chungungo is something we certainly want to try and adapt in other areas such as the Canary Islands, Cape Verde, Colombia, Ecuador, Guatemala, India, Israel, Jordan, Kenya, Namibia, Oman, the Philippines, South Africa, Tanzania, and Yemen. Even California and the west coast of the United States and Mexico might be good locations for this technology."

Surprisingly, the idea of using fog collectors to provide fresh drinking water is not new. While reviewing old research studies, Cereceda and her colleagues discovered that, in 1960, University of Northern Antofagasta physicist Carlos Espinosa had built nets to capture fog water. His work, in turn, was based on even earlier studies in other countries. Physicist Espinosa encouraged Cereceda and her team to continue this work. Together with anthropologist Horacio Larraín, the researchers were determined to put this idea into practice and spare thousands of people a lifestyle of poverty and illness caused by lack of water.

The experience gained during her work in northern Chile helped Cereceda understand the importance of having community involvement early on in any research project. "In Chungungo, we did not do this at first. It was our first experience; we were afraid of raising their hopes too high and then disappointing them. But when the community realized that we were trying to help them get water, we felt that they had come to understand that the water was for everyone and that it was an important resource they had to cherish and take care of. The participation of the community in learning to use water wisely and avoiding needless waste is obviously very important because the quantity of water collected is not limitless, it varies with the weather conditions."

The Camanchaca–Chile project, financed by IDRC and the Canadian Embassy in Santiago, had considerable scientific support provided by Professor Humberto Fuenzalida of the University of Chile and by the Institute of Geography of the Catholic University. CONAF Region IV was in charge of the technological part as well as the liaison with government organizations and the village. Currently, the Global Application Fog

Collection System Project is underway, and its aim is to take this technology and adapt it to other places in the world.

So who is this dynamic researcher who, with her team, has managed to achieve such excellent success with the fog-catchment project? As a young girl, Pilar Cereceda began her education at the Villa María Academy in Santiago, a Catholic school run by North American nuns. She acknowledges that her schooling gave her a working discipline, a mastery of the English language, and instilled in her a strong vocation for service. It is this third trait that has enabled her to overcome the problems involved in the activities of a research scientist. For Cereceda, the final goal is not science, but the people.

Cereceda comes from a family devoted to learning and knowledge. Her grandfather was Rector of the Federico Santa María Technical University, one of Chile's most prestigious universities. Her father, a medical doctor, was a professor at the University of Chile, and her uncle, a Jesuit priest, was a professor at the Gregorian University in Rome. Pilar Cereceda herself is a teacher of geography, history, and political science.

Author of more than a dozen books, on such topics as Chile's geography, environmental risks, hydrography, and the Chilean landscape, Professor Cereceda was awarded an Environmental Citation by the Canadian Meteorological and Oceanographic Society in 1993. She confesses that most fulfilling of all is "helping make possible the miracle of water, thus changing the quality of life of many families. Imagine what they feel like when, all of a sudden, they can take a shower in those desert areas where the summers are incredibly hot; what they feel when they cook their meals, clean their house, wash their clothes."

During her trips throughout the world, she has witnessed dramatic scenes, such as the one in Lima, "in the so-called *pueblos jovenes,* which are really nonurbanized plots of land that immigrants from rural areas take over. They arrive with nothing at all, build their houses with four straw mats, buy water from tanks, and store it in cans or steel drums for weeks on end. They use it and drink it, and it's probably contaminated by the same bacteria that cause the typhus and cholera epidemics that every so often occur in South America's poorest communities."

She has witnessed many people living in deplorable conditions caused by the lack of water. "I'll never forget a house we came upon in the coastal area of the Norte Chico in Chile. It belonged to a family of goat farmers: five adults and five children. Every 10 days they bought 200 litres of water. In other words, each one had 2 litres daily of water, barely enough for drinking and cooking. Not a drop was left over for personal hygiene, washing clothes or cleaning the house."

Another experience that deeply touched her was when, in the midst of the traditional water problems that assail Lima, Peruvian professionals set up fog collectors that now supply abundant water to a girls' school in the elegant La Molina neighbourhood. "I was moved by this because the water that now supplies the school caused a wave of solidarity and now that very same school is studying the possibility of installing more fog collectors, pipelines, and storage tanks to help the poor neighborhoods and the small farmers who live nearby."

In addition to her books, Professor Cereceda has explained her ideas and shared her knowledge on coastal fog as a hydrological resource and coastal fog applications at numerous seminars and conferences around the world: in Chile, China, Kenya, Morocco, the Philippines, and South Africa, among other places.

Her opinion on research for development in South American universities? "I think that, just like the fog-collector project, there are many more ideas, great research, in South American universities; projects that could be of great help to economically depressed communities. And all that's needed are nudges: one, so that the scientist or researcher would relinquish the peacefulness of the laboratory to find out how his or her ideas can be put to practice to help other people; and the second nudge, to encourage scientists to be constant in their quest for financing, when their own university is unable to provide it, by locating support from international institutions such as those of the United Nations, the European Community, Canada's IDRC, and others. Particularly useful are those funding sources that, in addition to financing the research, also provide incentives to researchers in their quest to find solutions to the real problems of the Third World."

Conducting research in South America can be difficult. "We normally lack more advanced instruments. Fifteen to twenty people share one secretary and a messenger boy, and we end up doing everything ourselves: from going out and buying pens and paper for the computer printer, to picking up deliveries at customs. But we have a great strength: that of our students and assistants who, brimming with youthful enthusiasm, prod us to achieve ever higher goals."

Her teaching role gives her immense satisfaction. She enjoys going out to the hills with her students and teaching them geography on site. "It is during field work where you can really enjoy the phenomena that we teach. In class, all you have is a blackboard, a transparency, or slide projector, everything is static. In the countryside you feel, you see, and you hear the phenomenon of nature. There you can talk, argue; you don't teach, you live the moment, and you share the natural event. When that happens, it's not the teacher who teaches, but the students and nature who teach the professor."

Why did she choose applied research? "As academics we spend too much time shut up in the ivory tower that is our university world. We retreat into our research so that the outside world won't disturb us. I always felt a force pushing me toward the people, to explain, in an easy manner, the technical job that we were doing. But, above all, what's most important for me is that the research we do is not left sitting there, but taken out to help people solve their problems."

In that pursuit, Pilar Cereceda has converted her experience into numerous slide shows and television films. She has also taught environmental protection and Chilean geography on the television education system, TELEDUC. In Chile, her project is acclaimed as "the first project from a Chilean university to be exported to other countries and benefit people throughout the world."

Devoted to research for the past 20 years, Cereceda's work goes hand in hand with that of Dr Robert Schemenauer of the Atmospheric Environment Service, Environment Canada, located in Downsview, Ontario. "Dr Schemenauer gave me the chance to enter the world of research at the highest level. I went to Canada in 1986, invited by the Atmospheric Environment Service and IDRC, to study the modern and sophisticated instruments used by the developed countries in their studies of rain and fog. It was quite a shock to compare them with what we use in South America. I also realized that we have many bad habits that we must change; for example, we take everything too slowly. This is a fast-paced world and we must adapt." Together with Dr Schemenauer, the Chilean professor is currently investigating acid rain on the Chilean coast and on Robinson Crusoe Island in the Juan Fernández Archipelago.

For thousands of years, people have survived trying to capture water from the clouds and the rain, without pipelines or canals, simply storing it in containers. Pilar Cereceda recalls that "according to a chronicler, about 200 years ago in the Canary Islands, the inhabitants used to collect water beneath a huge garoe tree. When the fog swept through the tree, droplets of water would trickle down the branches and the leaves, and every morning the women would go with their pitchers to get water. I saw similar systems in Oman, set up under olive trees.

On Easter Island, the locals pierced the volcanic rock and built virtual stone tanks called *tahetas*.

"And for ages, in the countries of the African Savanna, people have survived with 2 or 3 months of torrential rainfalls and 6 months or more of drought. What do they do? They collect the rainwater on their roofs and guide it to water tanks using the gutters. Even so, their water reserves only last for about 2 months and then the suffering begins: the thirst, the land dries up and stops producing food, the animals die, and sickness begins to appear."

The chance to get to know the most extraordinary people and cultures — in the midst of tedious instrument readings, calculations, and detailed analyses — is one of the reasons why Professor Cereceda confesses to an unconditional love of her work and of nature. She enjoys watching how the surroundings shape human beings: "how, depending on the way the wind blows, how it rains, the presence or absence of mountains, the quality of the land, the environment. All these determine whether people are happy or introverted, passive or active, selfish or ready to cooperate with each other."

In addition to her work as a professor at the Catholic University and other Chilean universities, Pilar Cereceda has taken part in over twenty research studies throughout the world sponsored by IDRC, Environment Canada, the Canadian International Development Agency (CIDA), and several Chilean and international organizations. Her work has included evaluation of ground-level ozone in two areas of Santiago, fog-water quality in Chile, development of international standards for measuring fog water, studies on the migrations of fisherfolk from Chile's third region, and acid rain and acid fog.

She has three children who are "great fans of mine. Two of them study journalism, and my 12-year-old daughter tells everyone at school all about her mother's work. I remember she used to cry because nobody believed her when she said she accompanied her mother to work in the clouds." Her oldest son has inherited her love of nature and today works on television programs about ecology and the environment. Her second daughter has acquired her mother's interest and talent for effective communication, and would like to become a writer; she also has a character very much like her mother's: happy and inexhaustible when she's doing something she likes. "My three children accompany me when I am doing field work and are real experts in my job."

Cecedres' dearest wish is to leave behind the pollution of the city and live in the countryside. She dreams of a more natural way of life and treasures beautiful memories of many trips. "In Chile's Fourth Region, there's a small village called Villaseca where the entire community uses solar energy with tremendous solidarity. It is fantastic to see the women take their pots off the solar grills at noon, which naturally do not contaminate at all. And you can smell the delicious *cazuela* [a typical Chilean meat and vegetable stew] everywhere in the village. To be able to live in the midst of such peaceful nature would be incredible, even though there are certain sacrifices involved."

She recalls research carried out in the Atacama desert, where she stayed for 10 days in a house with no electricity, no bathroom, and with earth floors. It was a village of some 150 inhabitants situated by a tiny stream. Surrounded by mountains, the villagers had laboriously built terraces into the hillsides like the ones built by the Incas. "My first impression was that this was far too remote and inhospitable: isolated, no services." Pilar Cereceda and the group that accompanied her decided that the best solution for this village was not to try to uproot it and move it closer to civilization but to improve the irrigation canals, modernize crop-growing techniques, and upgrade the roads.

"In other words, make their lives easier without moving them, leaving them with their peace and tranquility in the midst of nature. They are truly contented people leading simple and uncomplicated lives. They rejoice when a llama is born, when the harvest is good, when they celebrate the feast day of the village patron. They dance and sing to the Virgin in the traditional ceremony of *La Tirana*. How do they survive? By breeding rabbits and sheep, waiting for the rain and hoping that the year will bring a good harvest. Quite honestly, I have often thought of going to live with them."

Maria de Luigi is the recipient of numerous journalism awards and now writes for the newspaper La Epoca *and the magazine* Ercilla *in Santiago, Chile.*

JOYCE ROBINSON
(Jamaica)

Teacher, communications executive, and the first Jamaican to head the Jamaican Library Service, Joyce Robinson has contributed to the changing face of Jamaica during her lifetime. She led the national literacy campaign in the 1970s in which some 200 000 Jamaicans learned to read and write; and, from Unesco, came an International Literacy Prize for the campaign's excellent results. Although her honorary law degrees, lifetime achievement awards, and international travel opportunities are all very much appreciated, her greatest satisfaction comes from knowing that she has made a contribution to her country's development.

by Zadie Neufville

DR JOYCE ROBINSON HAS SPENT 52 YEARS IN THE FIELD of literacy, education, and training, and, although she is now retired, you would never know it to judge from her youthful appearance and her active daily routine. Her work has been recognized in her native Jamaica and beyond, and she does not lack for awards. She holds two honorary Doctor of Law degrees,[1] she is a Member of the British Empire, and, in 1979, was awarded the prestigious Order of Jamaica for outstanding public service.

Her career has had four distinct yet interrelated phases: library, literacy, television, and youth training. She started out in 1947 in library science and rose to become the first Jamaican director of the Jamaican Library Service. In 1973, she responded to a personal appeal from Prime Minister Michael Manley and assumed leadership of the troubled national literacy campaign. Eight years later, the campaign had taught some 200 000 Jamaicans to read and write, and she was awarded the Unesco Literacy Prize for its impressive results. A 1-year stint as General Manager of the state-owned Jamaican Broadcasting

---

[1] One is from Dalhousie University in Nova Scotia, Canada, and the other is from the University of the West Indies.

Corporation in 1982 was followed by 9 years as Managing Director of the HEART Trust, a national program designed to provide skills training to 17 to 25 year olds to reduce high unemployment.

An impressive body of work from a single individual, but hardly surprising to those who know her. Friends and colleagues describe her as "formidable": a woman known for consistently achieving her goals.

"Dr Rob," as she is affectionately known, began as a student teacher at 16 years of age and planned to study medicine. After completing Cambridge exams, Joyce worked voluntarily at the Young Mens' Christian Association (YMCA) in Trench Town before moving to the Black River High School in St Elizabeth. Her adoptive parents and Mrs F.E. Stewart started the school to provide affordable secondary education for St Elizabethans. The former high jumper taught five subjects at senior Cambridge Level and was games mistress before being appointed principal. It was while there that she became involved in library work.

After 3 years as a volunteer in the parish, Joyce was invited to join the Jamaica Library Service staff at its headquarters in Kingston. The climb through the ranks of the organization from Senior Assistant Librarian in 1947 to Director in 1957 was for Joyce, "enjoyable hard work." Within a span of 10 years, she became the first Jamaican Director of Library Service, the dreams of being a doctor long ago superseded by the "excitement of training to become a librarian."

There were no library schools in the Caribbean at that time, so young people wishing to become librarians took the external examinations set by the Library Association of Great Britain. Robinson became an associate of the library association in 1954 and, that year, won a British Council Scholarship to Northwestern Polytechnic in London, England. In 1959, she qualified as a Fellow of the Library Association.

Joyce entered the profession at a time when the influx of young, enthusiastic staff was changing the image of the library from the formal "custodian-of-books" image to a more socially relevant centre of knowledge and learning. "We felt we had to motivate the masses to read," she says of the early days, and credits the library service with encouraging reading habits at the broader level of society and inculcating reading for pleasure from school-age, which helped to reduce the high level of illiteracy.

Not everyone was pleased with such an active library service: many booksellers feared that a frequently used library would threaten book sales. Only one local bookseller had the foresight to recognize that a reading population would mean even greater book sales. "We convinced the booksellers that the library would only whet the appetite of readers, who would then want to buy more of their books.

"One feels very proud and very humble at the change that has occurred. I remember the days when 70 percent of Jamaicans who could read and write had no interest in reading for pleasure. Compare that to the present day, when Jamaicans are selective and discriminating in what they want to borrow from the library.

"We are proud of having arrived at a point where we now have books written by our own people, about our own culture. West Indian authors have gained international recognition for the quality of their work. We are proud of Derrick Walcott, a St Lucian and graduate of the University of the West Indies, who was awarded the Nobel Prize for Literature in 1993."

In the old days, libraries in rural Jamaica were boxes of books in the home of the volunteer. There was never enough money to pay staff, so the work had to be done by volunteers and the money spent on buying books and processing them for lending. "We utilized the human resources. By using people that children respected, we kept law and order and kept them bringing the books back, so we didn't lose books like we're doing now."

Strong "people skills" were required to run the library service. The challenge was to keep staff, clients, and volunteers motivated. It was the strategy of the library movement to involve every level of society in the library service. To keep volunteers interested, Robinson made sure they were invited to special functions and many received national awards. They were made to feel important.

More than a mere repository of printed reading material, the library was the centre of social life in rural communities. It was where many budding Jamaican artists had their first exhibitions. Master potter Cecil Baugh and famous Jamaican painter Karl Parboosingh first exhibited their work in libraries. "It was the only place children could go. Today, you have a lot of attractions but, in those days, the libraries were the only place," explains Robinson.

"Parents were a little hesitant. They said they didn't have time to read and come to the library. We had to convince them that we had books related to their interest or occupation. We would take a book with dress designs to a dressmaker and mount special interest exhibitions of books to attract and motivate target groups."

Robinson recalls that, even in middle-class homes, reading was not very popular in the 1950s. Back then, the Bible was the only book in many homes; but, by the 1960s, there was a vast improvement in book sales.

Robinson could never have developed the library service so well without the help of others, and she is quick to acknowledge that it was very much a team effort. Nothing could have been accomplished without the support of her staff, volunteers, and committees, she says. Many of those she worked with have gone on to become heads of libraries and some have remained her close friends.

Audrey Chambers worked with Robinson in the early years of the service. She was recruited straight out of grammar school after a family member spoke to Joyce about getting Chambers a job. Robinson knew the value of qualifications and, says Chambers, took the time and trouble to actively encourage others to take the Library Association exams.

Audrey later went on to university, and she never forgot Robinson's influence and the work of "those early pioneers of the service" as she calls Robinson and her team. "Indomitable" best describes Robinson, says Chambers, particularly the way she uses a subtle mix of persuasion and coercion to get the best from her staff, colleagues, and volunteers.

Norma Davis, another librarian who worked with Robinson agrees with Audrey's description of the woman many say almost single-handedly built the library service. Robinson believes her successes came as a result of the relationships she shared with her workers.

In 1957, Joyce married Leslie Robinson, a University Lecturer and then Head of the Mathematics Department at the University of the West Indies. By then, she was already head of the library service. Her husband continued a successful career to become the first Pro-Vice Chancellor of the University of the West Indies and the first Principal of the Mona Campus. Their son Anthony is a computer specialist and daughter Ann is a physican and consultant radiologist at the University Hospital of the West Indies.

Robinson and her husband have always had hectic schedules, but she organized her family and career so that both could be accomplished. It is the clock and diary that run her life. As she speaks, her alarm clock sounds. She explains that she carries the clock around so she won't miss appointments.

Joyce and Leslie Robinson are the only husband and wife team to have received individual awards of the Order of Jamaica — the Jamaican equivalent of the British Knighthood and Dame — a fact of which she is very proud.

The key to her successful integration of family and career, she says, was the fact that her husband was always in agreement with whatever she did. All important career plans were discussed in advance so they could be properly integrated with family life. Neither were ever away from home at the same time and, to compensate for the hectic schedule of their jobs, they made sure they took their vacations together.

Born Joyce Lawson on 2 July 1925, Robinson lost both her parents by the age of 6. Her father's best friend and his wife (Joyce's cousin) later adopted her. She speaks of the foresight of her grandmother who, she says, gave up her only grandchild so Joyce could have a better life. Among her prized possessions is the letter her grandmother wrote, thanking her "adopted father" for his interest and agreeing to the adoption.

Her family tradition is steeped in community service. Her natural father was a chemist, church organist, and community leader; her adopted father, a doctor. She recalls the many times he gave his service free of charge to those who could not afford to pay.

A hobby gardener, she tells of the days when she gardened at nights, as relaxation after a hard day's work. The high crime rate in Kingston has discouraged night gardening, but she still enjoys her plants by taking some inside with her.

The degrees, awards, and associated travel have all been welcome, but the best part of it all, she says, "is the satisfaction of knowing that you have made a contribution to your country's development." She takes pride in the fact that, through the Library Service and, later, the Jamaican Movement for Literacy (JAMAL), she was able to play a part in the development of rural Jamaica and the upliftment of the rural folk.

The library service experience prepared Robinson for the demands of the job as head of the revitalization of the national literacy program in 1973 and for the other jobs that followed. Robinson has the distinction of having worked with every

Jamaican Prime Minister since independence from Britain in 1962.

Robinson's nonpartisan approach to work is a trait admired by all. Few were surprised when, in 1973, the national literacy program ran into hard times, then Prime Minister Michael Manley asked Joyce Robinson to rescue the project that aimed at getting every Jamaican to read and write. One year later, in recognition of her individual personal contribution to maintaining a united Jamaica, Robinson was given the Unity Award.

During Robinson's 8-year JAMAL stewardship, over 200 000 Jamaicans learned to read. The success was largely due to the network of volunteers created along the lines of that used by the library service. Robinson and her staff used her library service contacts to maintain the network of 13 000 volunteer teachers, and 1 500 paid officers conducting 8 000 classes across the island. The network of community and church leaders and public- and private-sector officials was even more impressive when they succeeded in starting classes in the workplace. Team work, she says, was a very important component.

Early in JAMAL's reorganization, Robinson visited Cuba and observed its postliteracy program, which was effectively using radio to reach learners. On her return, she spearheaded the creation of radio and, later, television programs.

Joyce believes traditional ABC-type learning is not for adults. Programs developed specifically for adults should give them pride in their quest to learn to read and write to improve their lives. "It is rewarding when an adult comes up to you and says he has had a promotion because he learned to read and write," she says. She recalls, however, that in the early days people used to set their dogs on the recruiters who they believed were government spies.

Despite difficult times, JAMAL managed over the years to earn a reputation that removed the disdain with which the program was once regarded. Robinson is proud that she was a part of the system that "debunked" some of the old ideas about literacy. The literacy materials targeted the way of life of the people for whom they were developed. According to Robinson, people learn better if they are familiar with the subject and if they have attractive learning materials they can be proud of.

During her 8-year stint, over 100 titles were distributed to new readers free of charge. Robinson feels the program gained further recognition when, for the first time, a literacy student read the bible lesson at the opening of Parliament, a break with tradition and established constitutional procedure.

Televised quiz shows were later introduced, and these provided students with the incentive and opportunity to show off their new skills. Many students went on to sit for the General Certificate Examinations at the ordinary level. Some students went even further.

Robinson and her team promoted JAMAL as the advancement and development of the individual. Lanterns lit classrooms in areas where there was no electricity, and teachers were encouraged with awards and national honours, yet another tradition from the library service.

When she left JAMAL for the Jamaica Broadcasting Corporation (JBC) in 1981, Robinson had indeed rescued the Literacy Program. It won the Press Association of Jamaica special award for developmental work and, later, won a Unesco Literacy Award for its innovativeness and impact in increasing the levels of literacy.

Transformation was imminent for the government-owned national television and radio station, JBC. Then Prime Minister Edward Seaga felt that the job would best be handled by a non-partisan professional. As General Manager, Joyce was responsible for what was then the island's only television station, for JBC-AM and FM radio stations; and for television's transition from broadcasting in black and white to colour. She was also the first woman in the English-speaking Caribbean to head a media house.

"I was right back where I started. Only, for the first time in my life, I was negotiating with banks for huge sums of money," Robinson says chuckling. She describes the feeling as that which she experienced all those years ago when she first negotiated for land to build libraries.

Again, her library service experience was valuable when she was called on to negotiate transmitter sites, buy major equipment, and establish two additional part-time radio stations, JBC-Radio North East and JBC-Radio Central.

In 1982, she became Managing Director of the Human Employment and Resource Training Programme (HEART), a project out of Jamaica House (the office of the Prime Minister) to mobilize and offer skills training for school-leavers. In the 11 years under Joyce Robinson, the HEART Trust grew from a one-room facility at the Prime Minister's Office with one secretary and a part-time administrative assistant, to an organization with a budget of US $100 million providing training, development, and employment for over 30 000 young people.

Robinson saw the setting up of eight HEART Academies providing training for the hospitality, construction, cosmetology, garment, business, and agriculture sectors. The HEART school-leavers' program was also started to find training opportunities and placements in the private sector for young people who had left school with inadequate job skills.

Robinson also managed the implementation of the Solidarity Program. The project offered business training and granted loans through a self-start fund on the basis of character reference. At its inception, over 4 200 projects were established to help unemployed youths between the ages of 17 and 30 years. More than 35 000 people were assisted to become entrepreneurs.

When the program began, Robinson explains, labour unions and employers were skeptical. Unions felt their members would be affected, and companies were reluctant to employ unskilled personnel even if they would benefit from tax breaks.

Many contributed to the fund rather than take on the trainees, and money was used to set up training institutions.

The curricula at the eight island-wide academies consisted of 70 percent skills training and 30 percent life-coping skills, including reading, writing, and arithmetic. In an effort to place students, the HEART Trust worked with the Planning Institute of Jamaica to locate jobs.

Most academies were residential. "We couldn't train the young people and send them back at nights to the negative environment many came from until they were strong enough to survive," Robinson says. She believes her role was "to put a stamp" on lives of the young men and women and let them know the world doesn't owe them a living, that they owe it to themselves to find the doors that are open. One of the biggest headaches, she says, was the superior attitudes of trainers. "You had to let them know that a university degree doesn't make them better than the students."

Robinson and her management staff handpicked and trained academy teachers in acceptable cultural attitudes that would have a positive impact on the lives of the students. She explains that one of HEART's main concerns was improving the lifestyles of adults so they could be positive examples for the students.

Unlike many who complain about the differences between the older and younger generations, Robinson tries to strike a compromise. Although a strict disciplinarian, she doesn't want to make today's youth into her generation, she says. She sees them as generally a group of clean, healthy, if aggressive young people who are willing to work and achieve their goals.

Her biggest regret, she says, is that many of the excellent projects developed in the past 20 years have not had the sustained maintenance that would have allowed them to reach their full potential. Financial problems have all but crippled the Jamaica Library Service, but the foundation has already been laid for improvements and expansions in the system. Through

NACOLAIS, a system of referrals, library-to-library loans have been set up to ease the problem caused by a shortage of books.

"It pains my heart that, because of economic factors, volunteers are no longer available to serve as they once did." She regrets most the breakdown of the extended family.

Her rather piercing eyes have a twinkle, and her voice says volumes about the kindhearted person she is. One never leaves her home hungry or without a gift, no matter how simple.

The Jamaica Library Service has been the model of development for many other countries. It heralded a new era for libraries in the Caribbean. It created the need for a library school at the University of the West Indies, the establishment of the Jamaica Cultural Development Commission, and an appreciation for art.

With the exception of the Solidarity Program, which was later included into the Micro Investment Development Agency, all HEART academies and the HEART Trust still perform their original functions and now set the standard for vocational and skills training in Jamaica. Today, as it did in its early years, HEART places trainees in every sector of Jamaican society.

Although officially retired, Robinson still works 12 hours a day, much of it on volunteer projects. She offers services in nonformal educational programs, project planning and development, and library and literacy projects.

She still regularly receives letters, phone calls, and requests for various contributions of time and expertise. Robinson remains highly committed to those causes that involve education and training. Her deep sense of concern for the welfare of others is something she learned early in life. Service to others continues well into her retirement years because she feels that, after all, what is a life without some degree of service to others? "Service," she has said, "is the rent we pay for being on Earth."

Zadie Neufville is the agricultural reporter and subeditor at The Gleaner *daily newspaper in Kingston, Jamaica.*

Palmira Ventosilla
(Peru)

Microbiologist Palmira Ventosilla has developed a low-cost, environmentally friendly weapon in the fight against malaria in her native Peru: the weapon is coconuts. She readily admits that winning community acceptance of the program was even harder than the laboratory research. Since touring the Sierra as a youngster, Ventosilla has felt compelled to help improve the living conditions of her fellow Peruvians: her current work is helping to make a difference in disease prevention.

by Antonio Zighelboim

"WE HAVE BEEN USING DDT FOR 30 YEARS, AND NOW they tell us it is dangerous. If it is, it's about time we were told." Arturo Chiroque, a farmer in Piura, 650 miles north of Lima, is angry, suspicious, and impatient. Brother-in-law Hernan Hermosilla feels the same. "Now we hear that there are new ways to control malaria but that is hard to believe. And coming from a woman makes it very difficult to accept."

Skeptical comments such as these are nothing new to Palmira Ventosilla, 35-year-old Peruvian microbiologist, who, with her team of researchers, has developed a new way of controlling malaria. The method is one of biological control of mosquito larvae, but Ventosilla is the first to admit that winning community acceptance of the program was even harder work than developing the technology in the laboratory.

"This has not been an easy assignment," says Ventosilla. "Our natural enemy is the mosquito, but we also met resistance from the population with their deeply rooted beliefs. People are naturally skeptical because they are very close to their customs, and popular knowledge is paramount."

Piura is a neotropical region, and Salitral, the town where Ventosilla's program is based, goes from a very dry winter to a very humid rainy season, during which ponds form everywhere and act as breeding grounds for *Anopheles* mosquitoes. Over the years, local inhabitants have learned to live with the debilitating effects of the malaria (fever, chills, nausea, and muscle pain). But now, with the appearance of *Falciparum* malaria, there is a chance they may die of it.

What exactly is Ventosilla's new scientific breakthrough, and how was it achieved? Her idea began as a small component of a larger research proposal submitted to Canada's International Development Research Centre. It was Ventosilla's proposal for a community-based method of controlling *Anopheles* mosquito populations that attracted IDRC's interest, and funding was subsequently granted.

Ventosilla and her colleagues at the Alexander von Humboldt Tropical Medicine Institute in Lima began their research and soon learned about *Bacillus thuringiensis* var. *israelensis* (Bti) serotype H-14, a naturally occurring bacterium that is harmless to humans and animals, but kills *Anopheles* larvae. It is commercially available, but its cost can be prohibitive for developing countries. The team found a cheap way to produce Bti: growing it in coconuts and then releasing it into ponds where mosquito larvae flourish.

How does it work? A small amount of Bti is dropped through a hole drilled in a coconut. The hole is plugged with a wisp of cotton and sealed with candle wax. The coconut's hard shell protects the Bti during incubation, and the coconut milk contains the amino acids and carbohydrates the bacteria must eat to reproduce. After the coconuts have fermented for 2 or 3 days, they are broken open and thrown into a mosquito-infested pond. Along with their regular diet of algae, the mosquito larvae eat the bacteria. The Bti kills the larvae by destroying the stomach lining.

In tests, the Bti killed nearly all the mosquito larvae in a pond and stopped breeding for 12 to 45 days. A typical pond needs two to three coconuts for each treatment.

After the method was tested and perfected, the task of local community implementation began. Who in the community would carry out the mosquito-control program? The adults in the community were the obvious answer, but they presented difficulties: most of them did not want to contribute any of their scarce free time and energy to the program. Many were suspicious of this new program.

Ventosilla comments succinctly and with the candor that characterizes someone who has spent a great deal of time devoted to applied research: "It is difficult for outsiders even to imagine the environment we are trying to penetrate. This area lacks basic services; hygiene and health standards are rudimentary. People here do not like to be patronized or to hear foreigners tell them how to change their lifestyles. In our dealings with the local community, we have learned to proceed with understanding and care."

This sensitivity and concern for others has been part of Ventosilla's makeup from an early age. Born in Lima in 1959, Palmira traveled to Cerro de Pasco, in the Peruvian Sierra, when she was 7 years old. There she encountered the poverty and misery of the serranos. "All too often people would greet us with the widest smile, only to tell each other in Quechua, as soon as we turned our backs, don't trust *Limenos* [people from Lima]!"

These memories remained with her. In fact, when she chose biology as a major, a key factor in her decision was her desire to help the people she had met as a child.

Ventosilla first became interested in biology when she was in high school. She had been considering several career alternatives when she was invited to visit one of the most renowned private laboratories in Peru. "My grandmother had studied with Dr Hector Colichón, so when he learned that I wanted to decide on a major, he invited me over. It was love at first sight." As young Ventosilla toured the labs and looked through the microscopes, she knew she had found her vocation.

Pursuing biological research and seeing its potential for improving the human condition has led Ventosilla to appreciate the importance of closely involving the local community in planning and implementation. Although adults in Piura were skeptical about getting involved in a radically new program for malaria control, Ventosilla found that their children were keen to learn and participate.

An educational method developed by Ventosilla's colleague, Jorge Vélez, provided the children with clear information about the malaria, *Anopheles* mosquito breeding cycles, and Bti production. It had to be attractive and had to awaken the children's curiosity; therefore, Vélez designed posters, comic strips, and table games. "They seem to have liked it, their response was excellent."

At the same time, three other members of the team (Lucy Harman, Mark Snyder, and Esperanza Reyes) worked on a series of information sessions designed to reach the adult population. This was no easy goal. They had to convince the community of the potential harm, both to human beings and to the environment, of many chemical pesticides. They had to offset deeply rooted prejudices and assumptions. For example, the community was accustomed to waiting for government employees to come and fumigate houses and public places to kill mosquitoes. "Let the ministry do it," was a phrase heard over and over again. Adults were not very eager to accept that malaria could be regulated by controlling *Anopheles* larvae populations, as they were certain that the disease was something in the air in the fruit farms.

"Ecology is for the gringos. We have to feed our families, and do not have time for those things," said 24-year-old Maria Pérez. Children, on the other hand, proved to be brilliant teachers. After learning the technique, they took it home where they taught their parents and relatives everything they learned. They showed their parents that the method is inexpensive, very effective, and not time consuming at all. Eventually, parents began to pitch in and help.

Several short videos were made for use with the educational aspects of the program. "At first it was very difficult," offers producer Pedro Novak, who works with the team. "Rural people do not appreciate having a camera pointed at them. They don't like having their photographs taken, much less videos." The videos were used to launch discussions at community meetings where members of Salitral households participated.

"The meetings sometimes turned out to be very controversial," Novak adds, "but we could see that they were working. People began questioning their old methods and asking lots of questions." Community interest in the project has increased and more and more people are convinced, even those who had opposed the efforts made by "*la doctorcita*" from the very start.

The entire community has now been reached, and all three major schools of Salitral are ready to make room in their curriculum for the special biology course the program created. "Next year, we would like to cover more schools, more towns, and more ponds. Other communities are very interested in participating in this type of project," says Ventosilla.

"The ministries of health and education are helping us at the regional and local levels; however, it is the teachers who have been most receptive so far. We have won their confidence and support because we always allow them to review our educational material and give us their comments and approval. They appreciate it very much. We cannot hope to wipe out malaria completely from our country, because of the prevailing climate and terrain. But if local families are able to kill the mosquitoes in their backyard, the chances of them or their families contracting malaria become slimmer. And if their neighbours do the same, the probability keeps getting smaller and smaller.

"We need to prevent an epidemic," adds Ventosilla, "and the solution is in our hands, and in those of the community."

Antonio Zighelboim is a Peruvian writer and translator whose work has appeared in many of the newspapers and magazines of his country.

GUY COLLIN
(Quebec, Canada)

Guy Collin's work as a researcher has lead him to places he would never have imagined. Born in France, Collin found an adopted country in the beautiful Saguenay–Lac-Saint-Jean region of Quebec. As a chemical engineer, his expertise in the extraction and analysis of essential oils from local crops has taken him to Bolivia, Brazil, Morocco, and Rwanda. There, he discovered that marketing Quebec blueberry extracts has much in common with marketing lemongrass essence in Bolivia. The challenges facing this industry, both in Quebec and in the countries of the South, are not merely technological — they also involve the socioeconomic conditions prevailing in local communities.

by Bertrand Tremblay

THE UNIVERSITY OF QUEBEC AT CHICOUTIMI (UQAC) WAS only 1 week old when Guy Collin gave his first lectures there in the fall of 1969. He was firmly resolved to spend no more than 1 or 2 years in this remote region, far from major centres. He would stay just long enough to find a new job somewhere else.

A quarter of a century later, Collin holds the position of Vice Rector, Teaching and Research; his wife Andrée Parent teaches art part-time in elementary and high schools; and their two children, Isabelle and Pierre, are in medical school at Laval University, a field not offered at UQAC.

The Collins like their adopted country so much that they have never seriously thought of moving. Guy has found the university, with its 7 500 students, to be conducive to the flowering of his grand passion for research. The basic sciences team, which he still leads, does not limit its activities to the Saguenay Region; it is also active in Bolivia and in Africa working on projects supported by IDRC.

It was opportunity, chance, or circumstance, followed by a desire to see someplace new, which led Guy Collin from

Saint-Malo to the country of Maria Chapdelaine. While a student in chemical engineering at the Lyon National Institute of Applied Sciences, he had the choice, in 1964, of enrolling in one of France's "grandes écoles" or setting out on an adventure. Because he had always wanted to give up the comforts of his native land and travel far afield, at least temporarily, he took advantage of the opportunities offered by the exchanges between France and Canada. "My interest in exploring beyond my own borders won me one of the twenty scholarships that the Canadian government offered to French graduates wanting to study the Canadian phenomenon."

With a CA $3 000 scholarship[1] provided by the Canada Council, the young engineer spent 4 years writing his PhD thesis in chemistry at Laval University in Quebec City. While studying Spanish, he encountered a young Quebec woman, Andrée Parent, whom he married before the end of his time at Laval. After his years in the old capital of New France, Collin went to the National Academy of Sciences in Washington, DC, to do postdoctoral work; while there, he also worked on his English.

Armed with qualifications to join the workforce, the young doctor of chemistry submitted applications to numerous universities. The most interesting offer he received, worth CA $11 000, was from UQAC. He knew nothing of Saguenay–Lac-Saint-Jean and his wife had only once, as a child, ventured beyond the solid, 210-kilometre wall of coniferous forest that stretches between Quebec City and Chicoutimi in the Laurentians Wildlife Preserve.

Collin took on a wide variety of responsibilities at UQAC. He became Department Head and then Dean of Graduate Studies and Research in 1980. In 1992, he accepted an invitation to serve as Vice Rector, Teaching and Research. A first-rate

---

[1] At the time, $3 000 was equivalent to almost half the salary of some faculty members.

teacher himself, he considered program administration more a duty than a pleasure because research had always been his first professional love. When he first arrived at UQAC, Collin embarked on basic, "pure" research, divorced from socio-economic concerns; however, influenced by the expectations of the area and the pressures of his colleagues, he became increasingly involved in the extraction and analysis of natural products.

Guy Collin remembers the plant's early days: "In the 1980s, our team did systematic work on exploiting the commercial properties of the essential oils from some of the abundant conifers in the Saguenay–Lac-Saint-Jean area, with the intention of revitalizing a plant at Girardville, which was, for some years, one of the world's leading producers of essential oil from the black spruce."

When demand abruptly collapsed, the expertise developed in Chicoutimi caught the attention of the international applied research community, specifically IDRC, which was looking at a project to link Canadian researchers to work being done in Bolivia.

Researchers at the Universidad Mayor de San Simón (UMSS) had succeeded in extracting a sufficient amount of essential oils from the eucalyptus tree to meet the demand from local pharmacists. They had accordingly satisfied the domestic market for menthol, citral, and eucalyptol, which had previously been imported at an annual cost of US $700 000; however, they soon found themselves obliged to solve a number of problems to meet international standards and gain access to export markets. These oils, it should be noted, are the essential ingredients in the manufacture of detergents, soap, deodorants, and other household products; they represent a US $3.5 million market for Bolivia.

At this point, UMSS appealed to Canada for assistance. The Canadian government steered them to IDRC, which invited them to visit five laboratories. The one at Chicoutimi, known under the Laseve logo, scored highest.

Since then, the researchers at Chicoutimi have been involved in a two-part development program encompassing training and the supply of equipment for analysis and processing of essential oils extracted by distillation. These researchers have developed a raw-material processing technique, and UMSS is responsible for quality control of the product and adherence to marketing plans. This cooperation involves visits to Bolivia 2 weeks per year by Collin and his colleagues. Training is given at UQAC; four Bolivian students spent 6 months at Chicoutimi to develop their knowledge, while one colleague from the Saguenay spent 4 months training on the ground in Bolivia.

The agrochemical laboratory in the Bolivian city of Cochabamba, which has a population similar to that of Quebec City, requires a permanent staff of thirty — professors, engineers, technicians, a variety of teachers, secretaries, and truck drivers. They not only do work with essential oils. The varied make-up of the staff illustrates the range of the laboratory's concerns: it includes academics in the fields of food chemistry, chemical engineering, and industrial design.

Harvesting of vetiver, *Eucalyptus citriodora*, sweet fennel, romerillo, and thola has generated a genuine industry that is administered by agricultural cooperatives. The complex supplies a range of products: eucalyptol, whose antiseptic properties are used in the treatment of respiratory ailments; lemongrass, which is used in lemon candies; mint for menthol; pyretrius for insecticides; and a wide variety of other essential oils used primarily in the manufacture of perfume.

Bolivia's essential-oils industry exports approximately 10 tonnes of natural products annually, worth about US $150 000. A sum on this scale provides the means of existence for about 100 families in the underprivileged classes. The economic impact escalates as local entrepreneurs or new cooperatives take advantage of the opportunities that are offered to them for free.

The links forged over the past decade between UQAC and the harvesters of essential oils in the high valleys of Cochabamba, thanks to the stimulus of IDRC's financial assistance, represent a model for a truly effective contribution by an industrialized country to development in the Third World.

Bolivian researchers train staff and involve local communities in various stages of the program. They then encourage the cooperatives, or the individual peasants, when they become familiar with the technology, to buy distillation equipment with the money earned from the sale of the precious liquid. New entrepreneurs can thus move into downstream refining and processing operations, before they deliver their product to wholesalers who export it. Although the United States and Brazil were once the main consumer countries for eucalyptus oils, Germany now tops the list.

Guy Collin and his UQAC colleagues have achieved satisfactory initial results in their research into other plants. They have, in fact, managed to isolate new essences, and part of the production is purchased by French industry.

IDRC has, over the past decade, supported these projects, the goal of which is the development of one sector of Bolivia's economy. It was once hoped that Quebec industrialists would become involved in this research and development operation; this has not yet happened on a large scale. UQAC representatives have nevertheless acquired valuable knowledge that now enables them to understand why the Girardville experiment failed and to propose new approaches to the economic players in the Saguenay–Lac-Saint-Jean region. "We realized," explains Collin, "that the problems affecting development in this sector stem largely from the socioeconomic circumstances faced by local communities."

IDRC assistance, which is normally limited to 3 years, has already been renewed once in light of the outstanding results obtained by the team in Chicoutimi. If Canada grants further assistance, it will be under another program. Against this background, a colleague, François-Xavier Garneau, is currently working in Bolivia on the potential interest of certain medicinal plants. The Chicoutimi group is working on parallel projects in Benin, Ghana, Togo, and Rwanda, prior to the outbreak of violence. IDRC also entrusted Guy Collin with the task of coordinating the activities of a network of some fifteen African laboratories working with natural products.

The Girardville initiative between 1985 and 1990 resulted in the extraction of essential oils from black spruce, destined primarily for the cosmetic industry in the United States. The tiny company in Lac-Saint-Jean generated three part-time jobs and delivered a dozen or so barrels of oil, used mainly in soap manufacture, to a Montreal merchant. The company went bankrupt when the purchaser found a far cheaper source of raw material equivalent to the black spruce in the Siberian pine, which is abundant in Russia.

"This is why," Collin stipulates in his recommendations to local entrepreneurs, "we have to find products that are typical of this area and hard for foreign competitors to copy, such as maple syrup and blueberries." Donning his vice rector's hat, the professor from the Saguenay states that the emphasis is squarely on research that is relevant to the socioeconomic realities of the region.

Although this approach meets the demands of a population concerned about industrial change, it can also be explained by the difficulty, for universities of modest size, of sustaining competition in basic research with major institutions and specialized centres in Montreal, Toronto, and other large cities.

There are a few exceptions that prove the rule. The most obvious is La Société de Recherche sur les Populations, which, with its core of pure basic research, has developed a population index and competed successfully with major universities. The trick in outlying regions is to exploit market niches in which local researchers can have a relatively significant influence and contribute to stimulating the local economy.

"Our group believes that it can also effectively serve the student body, the scientific community, and local business people by becoming involved in the regeneration of the boreal forest," notes Guy Collin. "Several forest-products companies have already contributed financially to the project."

Newcomers to the Saguenay region will discover a society whose fabric is both rich and tightly woven. This was no different for the emigrant from Saint-Malo and his family. However, once the Collin children were in school, the whole family became closer to the community and the Saguenay–Lac-Saint-Jean hospitality.

Now, after a quarter century, Collin, his wife, and his children would never want to leave. They have come to love this brooding countryside dotted with lakes, rivers, and evergreen trees. The Collins have become genuine *"bleuets"* (blueberries), as the local people are called. They are part of that rich fabric of life that is Saguenay–Lac-Saint-Jean.

Bertrand Tremblay is founder and editor-in-chief of the bimonthly L'Activité économique *and, for 20 years, was senior editorial writer for* Le Quotidien *in Chicoutimi, Quebec.*

CHARLES SCHAFER
AND
JOHN NORTON SMITH
(Nova Scotia, Canada)

*C*ollaboration with Chinese scientists on research in support of the design and construction of new, environmentally safe harbours has given marine geologist Charles Schafer and marine chemist John Norton Smith unexpected rewards: a rich network of Chinese contacts, a fascinating cultural experience, and a sense of satisfaction that their capacity-building approach to collaboration will have long-term significance to China's future.

by Andrew Safer

A CHANCE ENCOUNTER IN 1985 WITH A VISITING Chinese scientist who was studying as a research fellow at Dalhousie University was a pivotal event in the lives of micropaleontologist Charles Schafer and marine chemist John Norton Smith, two research scientists working at the Bedford Institute of Oceanography in Dartmouth, Nova Scotia. Meeting with coastal geology researcher Professor Wang Ying — one of a select group of senior scientists sent to Canada for training by the Chinese government — eventually opened the door to an exciting new world of research, collaboration, and rich cultural experience for the two Canadians.

Professor Wang, a coastal geology expert from Nanjing University and winner of the All-China Woman of the Year award in 1985, had come to Nova Scotia in 1982. One day at the Bedford Institute she was excited to learn that a new type of electron microscope made it possible to extrapolate climatic conditions from the features imprinted on the microscopic surface of sand grains. That was the seminal beginnings of the China Harbours Siltation Project funded by IDRC.

According to Schafer: "We began talking while she was here, and we agreed, given all of the technology here, that we would try to put together a project that would put her university in the high-tech game of marine science." On a

6-hour train ride from Nanjing to Suchou, Schafer and Smith drew up the details of a preliminary proposal aimed at transferring technology to Nanjing University that would enable Professor Wang and her colleagues to conduct geophysical surveys and collect data offshore to provide a much-needed subtidal perspective for harbour-management strategies.

Unlike typical consultants, who would have devised harbour-development strategies for the local authorities, Schafer and Smith aimed to transfer their expertise to empower indigenous researchers to carry out the surveys themselves. "The idea was for us to become replaceable, and ultimately irrelevant," says Smith.

Micropaleontologist Schafer, 56 years old, specializes in mapping sediment transport in near-shore waterways. He studies the skeletons of microscopic marine protozoans, as they appear in sediment core samples, to determine the environmental conditions under which the sediments were deposited. Smith, 50 years old, works down the hall from Schafer and is an internationally known expert on the use of radioactive tracers to date marine sediments. He and colleague Katherine Ellis trained their Chinese colleagues and graduate students in sampling, data collection, and analysis. The lead-210 dating laboratory they set up at Nanjing University is still in use today.

With the financial assistance of IDRC, the Nova Scotia team organized the transfer of valuable technologies in the areas of reflection seismics and microwave navigation. They also taught their Chinese colleagues the basics of underwater geological surveying using scuba-diving methods.

In what ways did Schafer and Smith themselves benefit from the collaboration? When asked, they first mention the rich network of Chinese contacts, as well as a new context for their ongoing scientific work on coastal-zone issues. They also mention that they experienced the benefits of total immersion in Chinese culture.

"We were in China at a crucial time in the country's history," observes Smith, "when they were just starting to reach out to the West." Each year, when he and Schafer went back to conduct successive phases of the project, they witnessed dramatic change. "In 1986, everyone was riding bicycles and you still saw the occasional Mao jacket. By 1990, it was motorcycles and tailored three-piece suits." Schafer delighted in being able to "see the economic transition actually taking place" each time they returned to Hainan Island. "This is the exciting thing for us as scientists. We could go to a harbour that was going to be completely dug out, and we could look at the natural processes of the site both before and after development took place. These sorts of opportunities are rare in Canada."

Schafer and Smith learned that the Cultural Revolution had taken its toll on the lives of many of their Chinese colleagues. Reflecting on the turmoil caused during this dark decade, Smith observes: "Chinese scientists lost 10 years during the Cultural Revolution between 1966 and 1976. For a scientist, 10 years of no career is devastating."

Despite this setback, Schafer says it isn't much different working with the Chinese than working in a Western laboratory, largely because of their exceptionally high educational standards, particularly at the theoretical level. "Their capabilities on the theoretical side are astoundingly good."

The spirit of teamwork is very strong in China. Schafer recalls the time a large workforce was rapidly mobilized to erect the steel gantries on a ferry boat that was being converted into an oceanographic vessel for harbour surveys. The task was completed overnight. "One day, in a restaurant, I made some drawings and put some numbers on the back of an envelope," Schafer recalls. "That same day, about fifteen welders and workers arrived. Overnight, they did it all. When I looked at the ship from the hotel, it looked like a myriad of bright lights caused by the welders' arcs. They were simultaneously welding the pieces together. I saw about ten arcs all going at the same time."

Canadians are very popular in China, thanks to the legacy of Norman Bethune. "Recently, I found an English copy of the little red book," Schafer reports, "and in the section on Norman Bethune, he had been painted by Mao as virtually a God, an unselfish hard-working doctor. Many Chinese believe that Canadians all share Dr Bethune's qualities.

"I now realize that I underutilized my status as a Canadian working in China. I could probably have been more effective on behalf of my Nanjing colleagues in influencing decisions that were made as a result of the conferences."[1] His advice? "If you go to China, make sure they know you're a Canadian."

Although the China Harbours Siltation Project was a textbook case of technology transfer and transplanting research capabilities, Smith emphasizes the importance of an undercurrent that flowed throughout the project on a subtler level. He says that the Chinese had been taught to think linearly during the Cultural Revolution, and that the Canadian team's biggest contribution was to teach them to break out of that mould, to think creatively, and to be more flexible.

"That 10-year period, from 1966 to 1976, affected all Chinese scientists; they were programed not to think for themselves. They were taught to follow rules. Without being pushy, we tried to convince them that it is okay to be a little discordant and break a few rules. Professionally, this translated to helping them to develop the cross-fertilization required for multidisciplinary research."

Before they could be effective in their work in China, the Nova Scotia team had to learn the political setup and make friends with the local leaders. On their first trip to China, they were confused until they realized that there were two sets of bureaucracies — the Communist bureaucracy and the normal

---

[1] Nanjing University organized an international symposium that took place in the cities of Haikou and Sanya in 1990 to conclude the project and to introduce the results to the Chinese and international science community.

administration. "It did not take us very long to figure out that the Communist Party boss is equally if not more important than the professional administrator."

Although the Chinese are keen to find the balance between preserving the environment and fueling their economy, sustainable development often gives way to the pressures of rapid construction that outstrips planning. Schafer points to a US $1.5 million 100-room hotel that lies half built and abandoned because it was constructed 30 metres too close to the beach, in violation of Beijing bylaws. Schafer also recalls walking 100 metres from a high-rise building to a street where sewage was running in covered trenches. "The infrastructure isn't really keeping up with the rate of growth," he observes, noting that there are no traffic lights, no parking metres, and horrendous traffic jams on the streets of Haikou, Hainan's capital city.

"The magnitude of Hong Kong investment dollars being pumped into China is making the catch-up game all the more daunting," says Schafer. "With this sort of economic pressure, it's no wonder that the principles of sustainable development often fall through the cracks between government policymakers and private business interests.

"The understanding of sustainable development in China was fairly comprehensive at the national level," remarks Schafer, "and it was also well understood as a science concept at the university level. But at the local level, where people are out there constructing buildings and developing the coastline, it's probably not taken very seriously."

The harbours board and private developers are very receptive to advice because they seem to take a long-term view when it comes to preserving the natural environment. In fact, he recalls discussing the pros and cons of harbour development "to the point of fatigue" because the Chinese had seen that rapid development had created tremendous infrastructure problems in both Thailand and Malaysia.

Asked which side is winning the tug of war between sustainable development and growth in China, Smith said it is simply a function of how much people are exposed to environmental degradation and how much they want growth. As an example, he cites the discovery of mercury poisoning in Japan to show that people develop a sensitivity to an issue once it has directly affected them. "Hainan Island has had little prior development," he says. "Growth is far more important than environmental concerns."

Although Schafer is quick to say that "you don't change the world completely with a little project like this," he prides himself on having transplanted some expertise that is now paying dividends on Hainan Island. Professor Wang and her colleagues are currently using their new technological capabilities to conduct a large offshore seismic survey of a port approach channel north of the Yangtze River.

Has the project benefited Canada? Schafer says it has helped Canada to establish itself as a technology exporter within China's burgeoning economy. He predicts that new research projects would very likely involve private-sector participation, and that it is becoming increasingly important for organizations like Canada's Bedford Institute of Oceanography to establish international linkages that can help in developing new revenue-generating activities for Canadian industries.

As a result of the China project, Schafer's "real" ambition is to "learn as much about Chinese culture as I can before I die. I want to spend much more time learning the nitty-gritty about what makes that culture tick, and more about the history of that society. It makes me think that maybe I should have been an historian!"

Growing up, Schafer never seriously contemplated a career as an historian; instead, he had a strong bent for things mechanical. He admits to causing major electrical blowouts at home as a boy, the result of his curiosity-driven tinkering. Although mechanical gadgets sparked his interest in mechanical engineering as a teenager, his love of scuba diving led him to enrol in marine geology and natural sciences courses as a student at New York University (NYU).

After completing his doctorate at NYU in 1968, he joined the staff at the Bedford Institute, where he has worked on a variety of coastal, continental slope, and midocean, basin-marine geology projects. Schafer holds appointments as a Research Associate at Dalhousie University, an Adjunct Professor of Marine Sciences at Nanjing University, a Research Scientist in the Geological Survey of Canada, and as a Senior Scientist on various research vessels. He is also a member of the Board of Advisors of Nanjing University's State Pilot Laboratory. In 1990, Schafer was the co-recipient of a National Research Council of Canada Strategic Grant for a proposal that applies his environmental indicator techniques in aquaculture-impact research in eastern Canada.

Colleague Kevin Robertson, Technical Manager of the Environmental Marine Geology Subdivision at the Bedford Institute, has known Schafer for 27 years and says that he has a knack for becoming involved in projects before they become popular or well-known. "What I admire about Charlie is his foresight and his forward-looking vision. Whereas a lot of people have to be bribed with money and prestige before taking on new areas of research, Charlie is always there before them." Schafer, he says, was the first person in the department to become interested in aquaculture.

"But you won't see him get the glory for it," adds Robertson. "He doesn't go out seeking that. He loves science, and he likes doing things he thinks matter." Having been actively engaged in environmental research for some 30 years, Schafer now looks forward to leaving a legacy of scientific literature that his successors can further build on in the areas of nearshore sediment transport and the responses of near-shore ecosystems to climate change and contamination.

Research partner John Norton Smith, by contrast, admits that he has probably always possessed the making of a scientist from a very young age: a strong urge for independence and a drive for knowledge. "I didn't want to have limitations. The drive for knowledge was very important. And I wanted the opportunity to be creative and unbounded."

Smith received his doctorate in chemistry from the University of Toronto in 1974; the following year, the Department of Fisheries and Oceans offered him a postdoctorate in oceanography at the Bedford Institute somewhat by fluke. "I became a post-doc here partly because management misinterpreted my application," he explains wryly. "They looked at my experience, thought it pertained to radioactivity, and offered me the post-doc position in oceanography, which I knew absolutely nothing about."

Colleague Kevin Robertson says there was a certain excitement and fanfare surrounding Smith's arrival. "People used to tease him because he was the young guy, the golden boy, coming in. He was a pretty hot young scientist, and his success was very rapid. John was held in great esteem from the first days he was here."

After just a year and a half, Smith established a marine radioactivity laboratory to monitor the traces of radioactivity being released into the marine environment from the newly built Point Lepreau reactor in New Brunswick. Smith was among the first Canadian scientists to work with radionuclides in a macrotidal marine system and was among the first to perfect reliable lead-210 dating techniques.

Smith serves as Adjunct Professor at the University of Quebec at Rimouski and at Dalhousie University. He is also a Concurrent Professor at the Marine Geo-Sciences Department, Nanjing University, and Honourary Director of the Nanjing University Radioisotope Laboratory.

He is currently Head of the Atlantic Environmental Radioactivity Unit in the Marine Chemistry Division of

Fisheries and Ocean Canada and has served as Chief Scientist on more than fourteen major marine chemical expeditions.

What inspires his research? Smith said that much of it is driven by technology. "A lot of research evolves from data analysis, and recognizing that the data are not consistent with established models. For example, your equipment may become a bit more sophisticated and your lab technicians more skillful. With a more detailed database, new signals emerge from the noise. The interpretation of these signals often leads to new scientific insights."

Smith, whose group has been measuring radioactivity in the Arctic since the 1970s, cites a recent example: his research team measured extremely high levels of plutonium in a sediment sample taken from the Russian Arctic, which was later discovered to have been collected in a fjord where three Soviet underwater nuclear weapons tests had been conducted. "The other scientists on the ship were focusing exclusively on dump sites where radioactive waste had been deposited. Meanwhile, the plutonium contamination was far greater in this fjord than in the dump sites. Because we were interested in a broad understanding of the distribution of radioactivity in the environment, we were able to identify a potential source of contamination that may have otherwise gone undetected."

Asked what aspirations he has for future work, Smith replied, "What I'm doing right now is as exciting and challenging as it gets."

Andrew Safer, a Halifax-based journalist, has written more than 200 articles for newspapers and magazines throughout Canada, including Canadian Business *and* Computing Canada.

HANS SCHREIER
(British Columbia, Canada)

Mountain soil specialist Hans Schreier has been working since 1987 as part of a Nepalese–Canadian research team that is seeking solutions to the problems of soil degradation and deforestation. He admires the Nepalese people and way of life, and hopes that the research will help Nepal achieve more sustainable land use.

by Jo Moss

WHEN DR HANS SCHREIER PROPOSED INTRODUCING sophisticated computer technology into Nepal in the mid-1980s as part of a joint Canadian–Nepali project to evaluate the country's natural resources, it wasn't just other scientists who questioned his sanity. "There were a lot of skeptics," Schreier recalls. "Even I was pretty skeptical at the beginning. I wasn't sure if it would work."

A tiny mountainous country landlocked between the giants China and India, Nepal is one of the most impoverished and densely populated nations on Earth. The majority of its people are illiterate subsistence farmers eking out a living on terrain that Western farmers would ignore. Most of the country has no roads and no electricity, yet every square inch of land is squeezed into production. "It is probably the most intensely used country in the world," says Schreier.

At the same time, for someone like Schreier who grew up in Switzerland — another small country that also uses its land intensely — the Nepal project presented a challenge of a different sort: the opportunity to gather the first hard scientific data on Nepal's food, animal feed, and fuel resources and to find out if they were sustainable. In retrospect, he says, it was probably just as well he didn't know he would have to deal with problems like power shortages, poor hygiene conditions, monsoon floods, and earthquakes, not to mention the rocky political transition of a country going from kingdom to democracy.

"Failures? Oh yes, we had lots of failures," Schreier smiles. "Especially in the beginning. There was a lot of frustration but it got better. The thing is not to dwell on your failures, but on your successes." And the logistical problems? He shrugs. "You just become more flexible." When fuel shortages grounded their vehicle, he and other researchers took to bicycles, cycling muddy trails with soil samples on their backs.

A professor in resource-management sciences at the University of British Columbia in Vancouver, Canada, Schreier and his team work with Pravakar Shah, a Nepali scientist who did a graduate degree under Schreier and now leads the Mountain Resource Management Group in Nepal's International Centre for Integrated Mountain Development (ICIMOD). Schreier is quick to point out the success of the project is largely due to the enthusiasm of the Nepali research team. The synergy between the two groups has been the key to the project's success. Their collaborative work in the Jhikhu Khola watershed is now unique in the developing world in supplying data on deteriorating resources. It is both comprehensive and long term.

Beginning in 1988, Schreier has demonstrated that a personal-computer-based geographic information system (GIS) is an incredibly effective tool for managing resources in Nepal. For their part, Nepali researchers have proved themselves more than capable of handling the technology, despite the fact that none of them, except Shah, had ever seen a computer before or had any training in Western scientific methodology.

GIS was developed in the mid-1980s as a means of rapidly integrating different geographic data and assembling it into scenarios. Schreier quickly recognized it as an ideal means by which people working in different disciplines could pool environmental information for mutual benefit. He went on to pioneer its use in the developing world.

Initially, Schreier and Shah undertook what was the first major stocktaking of Nepal's land resources. They looked at deforestation, erosion, soil fertility, flooding, irrigation, and a number of other areas. By amassing the scarce information available and entering it into GIS, they were able to identify exactly how the land was being used for forestry and agriculture, and then to speculate on what activities were affecting which areas.

An 11 000-hectare area in the Middle Mountains, about 40 kilometres from the city of Kathmandu, was selected as the site for a more exhaustive survey. As a test site, the Jhikhu Khola watershed represents a worst-case scenario. It is one of the most densely populated regions of Nepal and suffers from excessive erosion and land deterioration. The research team set up field stations to collect resource data, trained local people to maintain the stations, and went from house to house in the watershed interviewing villagers about the pattern of their daily lives. Slowly and painstakingly, they built up a comprehensive data bank that showed the interaction between the communities and their environment.

Nepali farmers have learned to be innovative, constantly tinkering with their land to maximize productivity, even tripling crop rotations. The problem is that the population is now doubling every 25 years and, for the first time in its history, the country is reaching its limits. "Nepal is heading for a crisis, there is no doubt about it," Schreier says. "It's reaching the point where it is no longer sustainable." He and Shah are trying to demonstrate how GIS can be used not only to identify problems but also to find sustainable solutions.

Schreier's field research took him into remote areas where he was the first Westerner villagers had ever seen. "It is not unusual to be greeted by twenty curious villagers, all standing close and wanting to touch you," he says. He experienced hair-raising trips on Nepali buses crammed to the roof with families, animals, and household goods. It has also meant rolling up his sleeves, picking up a spade, and doing some hard digging. It's all part of getting the job done and a part of the work he obviously enjoys and recounts with relish.

The team's early findings overturned a widespread belief in the rest of the world that Nepal's forests were declining. Research showed, instead, that the forest was expanding and it was fuel wood and animal fodder that were rapidly being exhausted. They also found that although reforestation efforts had replaced half the forest land lost since 1947, the wrong kinds of trees (pines) were being planted extensively and on the wrong sites. Pine needles make the soil less fertile by increasing the acidity, and pine trees are not as good for firewood or animal feed as other species. Because the pines were planted on intermediate rather than steep slopes, they have done little to prevent soil erosion.

Although forest cover is increasing, it is having a negative impact on other resources. The group is now using GIS to select a "super tree" that is native to Nepal and would be more useful to villagers. Trial nurseries have been set up with local farmers who have been enthusiastic participants since the beginning of the project.

This is the aspect of the work that Schreier finds most exciting. Modest about his own accomplishments in the project, Schreier becomes animated and enthusiastic as he talks about the potential of the team's efforts. After 7 years, the study has finally reached a stage where some of the results can be translated directly into practical projects. "We have struggled for years," he says. "Now we can seriously start looking at how we can influence the system to bring about change."

Many of their projects he describes as "off the wall", but says that the freedom to try out different things is what makes it fun. The group is looking at ways, for example, to reclaim gullies for agriculture, conserve water with a novel trickle-irrigation method, reverse soil acidity, improve honey production, and determine the viability of watermelon and cucumber as cash crops. Schreier is unequivocal in his view that this work is the most challenging thing he has done in his life.

The researchers are constantly revising their plans as new situations present themselves, and many of the project ideas evolve as a direct response to local needs. For example, when they brought in solar panels to recharge the car batteries used to run the field computers, they soon realized the potential to provide a cheap source of electricity to nearby villages. One community wanted a suspension bridge so they could have access to the rest of the valley during the monsoon season; the bridge would also make access easier and safer for researchers collecting hydrometric data. So an agreement was struck whereby the researchers would provide construction materials and the villagers would provide the labour. It was completed entirely by the Nepali team, in record time and at minimal cost, much to everyone's satisfaction. "I'm very proud of this bridge," says Schreier.

Schreier began his career in organic chemistry and worked in the pharmaceutical industry before making a somewhat unusual switch to a specialization in soil and water analysis as a geologist. He joined the University of British Columbia in 1978 and immediately helped set up a new resource-management program that brings scientists from different fields together for environmental research. He is a strong proponent of the interdisciplinary approach that, as far as the environment is concerned, he believes is the best and, indeed, only way forward. "Everything is so interrelated and the problems are so complex that we have to start operating in teams," he says.

The concept of sustainable development is a relatively recent one, even in the scientific community. It was a trip to the Soviet Union in 1989 for a conference on mountain ecosystems and a visit to the province of Tajikistan that was a turning point for Schreier. "It was just unbelievable, the environmental problems relating to industrialization, and in such proportions. I thought I knew what was going on in terms of land degradation. Perhaps I was a bit naive, but I was shocked." The Soviets, meanwhile, were so impressed with GIS technology, that Schreier was invited back the following year to show how the technology could be applied to their needs.

Schreier's involvement in other development projects has taken him to Chile, China, Columbia, Ecuador, Peru, the Philippines, and, most recently, Egypt. But he says it is Nepal that has been the most fascinating and most rewarding place to work. His personal involvement and enthusiasm is more than evident, and his description of the country and its people is always in superlatives. "It is the most incredible place and the people are wonderful. You get hooked on this country."

That wasn't his first impression, however, when he arrived in 1988 at the end of the monsoon season. He arrived with his wife and 7-year-old daughter and took up residence in a tiny two-room house on the edge of the ricefields in the Jhikhu Khola watershed. "We came at the wrong time of year and it was very difficult," Schreier recalls. Sanitation was nonexistent, all the water had to be filtered, and there was little to supplement a basic rice and lentils diet. "It wasn't easy to adjust, but it got better." Then he grins. "Now we look back at it and think it was great." What shocks Westerners the most about Nepal is the grinding poverty and backbreaking labour, especially for women. "Every time I go I still get culture shock," he admits. "You go over two valleys from Kathmandu and it is like stepping back in time to medieval Europe."

Over the past 7 years he has seen the country change dramatically as Western goods such as cars and television have poured into Kathmandu. His experiences have brought him very close to Nepal and its people and although the changes may be inevitable, he finds them disturbing. He believes the only two options now open to the struggling country are to take control of and develop its tourism industry as a source of foreign income and create a market economy that would alleviate poverty in remote areas. Both would radically alter what has, up to now, been a cashless society. Both require a tremendous social adjustment by the people and the Nepali government. That's the part he's not so optimistic about. "I am trying to be optimistic, but it's hard," he says.

Now an energetic 54 year old, he readily admits Nepal has changed him over the years. "I've become more philosophical. You come to the realization that everything takes time. You can't expect things to happen right away, you have to become more patient, although I'm not a very patient person."

Doing research in a developing country is not for everyone. Beyond requiring a certain physical hardiness, there is the frustration of coming up with hard scientific facts under adverse conditions, most of which are totally beyond your control. Flexibility is a word Dr Schreier uses often. Along with optimism, he believes it's an essential attitude to adopt. "You know there are going to be so many logistical and political problems, so you try to do as many things as possible, knowing that some won't work and others will. That's very different from what we do in Canada," he says.

Schreier's and Shah's work in Nepal is somewhat unusual not only in its direct grassroots approach but also in terms of the length of time the project has been underway. "Seven years is a luxury, and it shouldn't be," says Dr Schreier. "We are just now starting to appreciate and understand the dynamics of the system and how it's evolving." Part of the work the researchers are now doing, for example, is measuring the villagers' perception of their environment. Nepali farmers have an intricate land-management system that, at first glance, may seem haphazard, but becomes more apparently deliberate as researchers learn more about the natural resources and Nepali society.

Nepal is a mixture of Buddhist and Hindu populations and Schreier finds much to admire in this family-oriented society where people's lives are hard, but where the community works together for a common good. He admits he still doesn't understand it. "There are so many taboos." As for the complex caste system, "I'm hopeless at it." Although the Canadian researchers are sensitive to local culture and customs, they do some things Nepalis find quite astounding. Women, for example, are included in the project as paid workers and team members. It is a concept that has no place in Nepal, where females have a clearly defined subservient role in a male hierarchy. "We try and incorporate anyone who is interested," Schreier explained. "And I don't know if it's right or not, but we do try to set a kind of example."

After working in the watershed for 7 years and involving local villagers in every aspect of their work, Schreier feels they have finally been accepted by the watershed communities, a rapport that is a welcome bonus and an essential factor in the project's success. "They see we are interested and sincere about what we are doing," he explains. "We aren't just passing through." The villagers also see Westerners and high-caste Nepali researchers, who normally wouldn't do manual labour, getting dirty and sweaty doing physically arduous tasks. It earns them a great deal of respect. Far from being traditional, local farmers are quick to take up the new ideas and exploit them for their own use, and Schreier is full of admiration for the way in which they have taken up aspects of the research. "Once they take the initiative, it is wonderful; there's no stopping them. The only thing you have to do is try and slow them down."

The Jhikhu Khola watershed project is small, but the team is doing all it can to train Nepalis in applying GIS technology and to share its findings, both formally and informally, with local people, government administrators, and international agencies. Here, GIS has proved to be a novel education tool because information can be displayed visually on a portable screen. Schreier says its effect on viewers is magnetic. The team's ultimate objective is to create a pool of local expertise with the skills and technology to manage the country's resources effectively. Now that the project has established somewhat of a reputation, visitors to the watershed are frequent, but Schreier qualifies the overall impact the project has had. "In development terms, what we are doing is a drop in the bucket," he says ruefully. "But someone has to do it; I guess that's why Shah and I are still there."

His varied involvement in developing countries has made him adamant that sustainable planning for resources in those areas cannot hope to be successful without long-term monitoring of the resources, by which he means over 6 to 10 years. "You have to take a long-term view," he argues passionately. "How can we go in with technology for development when we don't understand the land and the natural systems? And, worse yet, we don't understand anything about the social system, which is probably more important to understand than anything else. Without test sites supplying this kind of data, it's so easy to make decisions that are totally inappropriate."

Schreier points out that scientists have had little experience in rehabilitating natural resources, which should make conservation the more logical of the two available options. Rehabilitation is a challenging task requiring a great deal of creativity, he explains. Most people don't realize it can take as little as 2 years to destroy a soil system, but up to 30 years to rehabilitate it. "If you have a good producing system you can sustain it and maintain it with little effort, but once it's gone...," he gestures helplessly.

"We have had lots of experience destroying habitats, and almost none creating them. The cost and time is horrendous. It's a hell of a job."

Jo Moss began her career with CBC radio in Vancouver and recently completed a stint in London, England, where she reported on commonwealth and international-development issues.

Patricia Stamp
(Ontario, Canada)

*P*rofessor and author Patricia Stamp was a founding member of the Women's Studies and African Studies programs at York University in Toronto in the early 1970s. Born in England and raised in South Africa, she has traveled throughout Africa and Asia as part of her gender and development research. Through her work, she has helped increase understanding of Africa, especially African women, and continues to promote greater collaboration among Third World and Western researchers.

by Kirsteen MacLeod

TAKING THE FLOOR TO ADDRESS THE WOMEN'S Education and Research Centre in Colombo, Sri Lanka, in June 1994, Patricia Stamp's belief in the spirit of *ngwatio* was apparent. *Ngwatio*, in the language of Kenya's Kikuyu ethnic group, originally meant collective cultivation, women joining together to weed one another's fields. Now it refers to different types of collaborative work.

As a passionate advocate of collaborative research in the Third World, Stamp decided that, in the spirit of working together, she would provide the women with a rare opportunity to reverse the gaze and take a good look at a Western feminist.

"Third World women have offered themselves for scrutiny, wittingly and unwittingly, for a long time," says Stamp. "It's time for us Western feminists to show some reciprocity." With characteristic openness and sensitivity, Stamp, a noted academic and Africanist scholar, then proceeded to give telling details about her personal life, work, ideology, and influences.

"The reason why I am baring my soul to you is because I feel that revealing my provenance to your scrutiny is directly related to the whole question of comparative Third World research; collaboration between Third World and Western scholars; and, above all, the accountability that Western scholars have to their Third World colleagues and the subjects of their research," Stamp explained.

The 6-week Sri Lankan visit was part of a sabbatical research project on "Women, Democracy, and Development: A Comparison of African and South Asian Cases." Stamp had previously spent 2 months in Ghana, West Africa. In each country, she collaborated with a local researcher. Funded by the Social Sciences and Humanities Research Council of Canada, the end-result will be a book and, perhaps, with additional funding, a presentation at the International Women's NGO Conference in Beijing in 1995.

The project is the latest development in a life-long dedication to academia. Stamp is 51 years old and an Associate Professor of Social Science at Toronto's York University. She is affiliated with three graduate programs: social and political thought, political science, and women's studies. She came to her current focus on gender and development studies out of her ongoing work in African politics and ideology.

Stamp's enthusiasm for her work — she has been an Africanist scholar and activist for her entire adult life — is as contagious as her credentials are impressive. She was a founding member of the Women's Studies and African Studies programs at York in the early 1970s, and, in 1991, she founded its Development Studies Resource Centre.

Stamp's work — "an intellectual passion, as well as a strong political commitment," as she describes it — has taken her far and wide. At times, her hybrid-accented voice attests to her previous homes in North America, Britain, and Africa. Since 1969, she has done fieldwork and comparative research throughout Africa and Asia. Stamp is best known for her work in Kenya, where she has lived and visited frequently over the years. She is the author of many articles and papers on Kenyan politics, society, local government, gender relations, and development.

Her work has influenced many in the West and in Africa, with its emphasis on grassroots participation in research and use of local knowledge. She has encouraged many scholars to take the use of case studies more seriously. Her best-known work is a pioneering book published by IDRC in 1989 called *Technology, Gender, and Power in Africa*,[1] which is currently in its third printing. Stamp laughingly dubs it "the Coles Notes of development and gender relations," because it links the relatively new fields of gender studies, African studies, and development studies. Stamp stresses that concerns such as the invisibility of gender must be taken into account in development research and planning, and it is the role of scholars and development agents to ensure this happens.

As a researcher in Africa and other Third World countries for the past 25 years, Stamp has developed the expertise necessary to clearly trace the complicated interrelated factors that hinder development efforts. She challenges everything from Western assumptions about the applicability of accepted Western economic, political, and gender concepts in non-Western contexts to the devaluing of empirical research in the current era. She stresses the need for technology not to be seen as neutral objects, but as value-laden social constructs of Western society. Computers or fertilizers are seen as social, not physical objects.

The book, with its detailed exploration of the relationship between technology, power, and gender, shows how for most women in the developing world, technology has failed. In Africa, women are largely responsible for agriculture, health, and nutrition. Technology — usually health-related, such as those aimed at nutrition, control of reproduction, and improvement of child care, or agricultural-related, including mechanization, pesticides, and genetic engineering — has often hindered, not helped, development in Africa. Often, with the introduction of technology, women's position in the family has become more

---

[1] Stamp, P. 1989. Technology, gender, and power in Africa. International Development Research Centre, Ottawa, ON, Canada.

subordinate; they have lost resource rights, and, in addition to interfering with their ability to take care of their traditional responsibilities, technology has only increased their workload.

Stamp shows how this problem has arisen from Western notions of what people in developing countries want and need, as expressed in the technologies they provide, and articulated in conceptual frameworks not appropriate for Third World societies.

"I am on a lifelong crusade about valuing indigenous knowledge, rather than crushing it under heel with so-called expertise and know-how. Not just Westerners, but some educated people in the Third World too, look down their noses and say you need to do this or that, or you don't know how to do anything." She says this notion of backwardness in Africa infuriates her, as it ignores the obvious wisdom of local practices.

"The Maasai, for instance, are incredibly sophisticated politically, economically, and socially, and they do it without television, electricity, and modern gadgets. Their material life is so simple, and the rest of their life is so complex. For example, their cattle management and dairying procedures are scientifically based on their own observations over thousands of years."

Stamp's own pioneering path, making multidisciplinary links among Africa, gender, and development, has been forged bit by bit by personal and professional forces over her whole life. Stamp's family on her father's side was part of the British intelligentsia; her grandfather was leading economist Sir Josiah Stamp, who wrote books with John Maynard Keynes; and her godfather was Dudley Stamp, author of ground-breaking books on world geography in the early 1900s.

"On my Dad's side, there was the idea of service, of being an academic and intellectual," she says. She did not grow up in England with the rest of the Stamp clan: father Colin Stamp took his family to South Africa in 1947 to open the first American Express office in Africa, and he later worked in travel broadcasting, which instilled a sense of adventure in his daughter.

"The pride of my young life was to tune in every Sunday to the South African Broadcasting Corporation's *Abroad on Sunday Morning with Colin Stamp*, where he would tell anecdotes about his travels," Stamp recalls. She remembers fondly how her father "out of pure idealism" took off into the bush to spend 2 weeks with Albert Schweitzer, one of the best experiences of his life, just to see what the great man was up to.

From both sides of the family, she inherited a "lifelong marginalization." The feeling of being an outsider is a legacy that Stamp values: from it she learned to develop independence in her politics and ethics. "I always felt marginal, the overseas colonial contingent of the Stamp clan," she says. "And I never had a chance to speak to my Chicago family who did illustrious things: my mother was the stepdaughter of an aristocratic Chicago family, but I was never a part of that."

Stamp's mother, Althea, was a strong influence. "She inculcated a sense of fearlessness in me and my sisters, the feeling that women really can do anything." For several winter holidays in a row, Althea would pile her teenaged girls into the station wagon, "a huge Plymouth with great big tailfins, laden down with all our gear," to explore the south and east of Africa for weeks at a time. "Friends would say to my mother: 'How could you be so irresponsible, there is rioting in Salisbury, Mau Mau in Nairobi, how could you take your kids to darkest Africa?' Then, when we got to Salisbury [Harare today], they'd say: 'You've come from Johannesburg, it's dangerous down there!' "

These safaris were Stamp's first introduction to East Africa, where she was later drawn and concentrated her research efforts. Although she was born in Cornwall (in a nursing home where her mother was staying to avoid the bombing during World War II), Stamp says she doesn't feel British. And, although she lived in the United States, she says she doesn't feel American either. When it came time to go back to Africa, she says she didn't belong in the segregated life of South Africa. Instead, she headed for newly independent East Africa.

She considers Africa her spiritual home. "I do feel in some way I am an African. If it is possible to become an African, to be transformed into a person of a certain place, then I am. I'm a white African, and I belong there, so I'll go to the place where my energies can be optimized."

Recent changes in South Africa bring her deep joy, from a political, as well as a personal standpoint. Throughout her life, Stamp has faced the widespread North American view that anyone white from South Africa must have been colluding with the white regime. Her desire to study African politics and her passion for justice are, she speculates, in part a reaction to her rage in finding as an adult that her childhood as part of a privileged community was predicated on the oppression of others. "I was flaming angry when I grew up and discovered that the innocence of my childhood was premised on apartheid." Although her parents were not political, Stamp says they were angered by injustices. She remembers her mother giving lifts to blacks during bus strikes in her station wagon, then getting arrested for her efforts.

Stamp's youth in South Africa at the time when the Nationalist government was really institutionalizing apartheid also provided her at an early age with the ability to be comfortable with discomfort, to accept the contradictions of belonging to an oppressive class whose ideology one despises.

"This is the bedrock upon which I build my politics and understanding," Stamp says. "I want to avoid being one of those middle-class progressives flagelating themselves for the class they were born into. I think that acceptance of contradictions has sustained me, especially now as we are going through an era of identity politics. Whites are made to feel white guilt, but I personally feel that white guilt is self-indulgent. It is very easy to feel uncomfortable and then forget about it. It is much harder to accept your contradictory position and then try and do something about it."

She left South Africa to attend Wellesley College in Massachusetts in the United States, where she obtained her BA in political science in 1965. Stamp later returned to London, England, gaining her master's degree in African politics at the London School of Economics in 1968. Her examiner was great Africanist scholar Colin Leys, for whom she worked as research assistant in Kenya. Later, she conducted her doctoral research in Kenya while teaching full time and received an external doctoral degree from London University with a dissertation on municipal politics in Kenya entitled "Governing Thika: Dilemmas of Municipal Politics in Kenya."

As a researcher in Kenya in her mid-twenties, Stamp picked up where her mother's safaris left off: in addition to conducting research and teaching at the University of Nairobi, she was a travel guide for a while, flying all over Africa and taking slides. She bought a Mini Minor, camped in the bush, made friends with East African ecologists, and became an avid birdwatcher and amateur biologist.

By the early 1970s, Stamp needed to earn some money and wanted to return to North America. She wasn't keen on returning to the United States, but had heard good things about Toronto. She came and knocked on doors and eventually landed a sessional lecturer job at York University in 1971. She has taught there ever since, achieving tenure in 1979.

Stamp spent the next few years teaching, with summers in Kenya doing fieldwork on municipal politics. While teaching a summer course in the north of Kenya in 1973, Stamp met an interesting young York anthropology major, whom she later married. Stamp and Stephen Katz, now a Professor of Sociology at Trent University, have a home in Toronto's Willowdale, which is decorated with African art and has bookshelves lined with lovely old books on Africa. Their 17-year marriage made Stamp's connection with Canada a permanent one.

Out of her work on African politics and ideology came her involvement in gender and development studies. With the birth of women's studies in the 1970s, Stamp was on the forefront of the struggle to have it inserted into various disciplines. When she attempted to teach a course giving a comparative approach to the study of women, with a special focus on Africa, it became clear that women were as invisible in literature on Africa as they were in other areas of social research.

In the spirit of *ngwatio*, Stamp started collecting materials for the new women's studies course at York while she was doing fieldwork for her doctorate in the summer. Out of the lectures, seminars, and student essays, certain questions arose, ones that Stamp is still exploring. Did women have more power and autonomy in the past than they have today? Under what conditions? Does women's power and autonomy ever persist in the present and, if so, how? How do women themselves perceive social change and organize a response to it?

In 1974, for her first gender-relations research, Stamp received a grant of CA $750 to fund a research project to study Kikuyu women's self-help groups in Mitero, Kenya, a small rural area close to the town where she was conducting her doctoral research.

It was the type of collaborative research that has informed her work ever since. As she and her long-time friend and associate Rebecca Njeri Chege, currently supervisor of family welfare in the Nairobi city council, explain in their article, *Ngwatio: A Story of Cooperative Research on African Women*,[2] the research questions and methods were guided by the village women.

Stamp — who is godmother to Chege's daughter and describes Chege as "a very important part of my life and an amazing woman" — began working with Chege in 1974. Chege, then a social worker in the town of Thika, also joined her in her research again in 1981 and 1985.

---

[2] Stamp, P.; Chege, R.N. 1984. Ngwatio: a story of cooperative research on African women. Canadian Woman Studies, 6(1), 5–9.

Burying Otiena[3] is considered one of Stamp's finest pieces of gender-relations work. It analyzes the relations between gender, class, and ideology in Africa. In it, Stamp has provided a fascinating account of the trial of a Kenyan widow who was taken to court by her dead husband's family for possession of his remains, and who lost custody of his body because they were from two different ethnic groups. The article outlines the complex forces that cause the widow, who is of the Kikuyu ethnic group, to lose the right to his body to the Luo clan of her husband, Otieno, so they can bury him according to Luo custom. The sensational trial, which took place in 1987, brings up issues of customary versus common law, women's rights and why there was no effective feminist challenge, and intertribal marriages.

Stamp says she grew into her own brand of feminism as Africans grew into theirs. The theoretical and ideological divides are not between African and Western feminism, but within the two, she stresses. African feminism does differ from Western feminism in some key areas. For example, Africans tend to see the collective nature of culture and reject the individualism of Western feminism; they also reject the Western feminism that often focuses on antagonistic male–female relations.

This reflects Stamp's viewpoint. "My feminism evolved in the context of my experience as an Africanist and my own self-identified way as an African. So, from the start, I had an allergy to the separatism of the Western feminists because of my belief that, yes, we want to see a correction of women's position in society, justice and so on, but not because all men have oppressed all women for all time."

Stamp's research bears out her belief that women in Africa had more powerful positions in the past and that colonialism and the forces of capitalism have eroded that. "Mothers of Invention: Women's Agency in the Kenyan State," a

---

[3] Stamp, P. 1991. Burying Otiena: the politics of gender and ethnicity in Kenya. Signs, 16(4), 808–845.

forthcoming chapter in *Provoking Agents: Gender and Agency in Theory and Practice* (University of Illinois Press), illustrates that women — contrary to the view disseminated in much women-in-development and Western feminist literature — are not unresisting, but are actually using their self-help groups as well as their actions on the national stage as agents of change, to try and stem their loss of power, eroded by colonialism and capitalism.

Stamp says the highlight of her sabbatical last year was the collaborative work, because it recharges her, and keeps her optimistic. She is a dynamic, warm and infectiously energetic woman, but admits that, at times, the struggle for change can seem an uphill one. Esther Ofei-Aboagye, a faculty member at the Ghana Institute for Management and Public Administration in Accra, co-organizer of a workshop on empowerment held at the Presbyterian Women's Centre near Accra in March 1994, says that Third World women also get charged by such information exchanges as the one that went on between her group and Stamp.

"Patricia's work and the collaborations she has done are a good example of cross-cultures — how people can exchange and benefit from one another," says Ofei-Aboagye. Stamp provided valuable services as a transcriber of the conference proceedings and as external evaluator, to talk about what worked and didn't work, and give insights on the conference as Africanist, expert, and academic. Stamp herself got the chance to enrich her ongoing work by participating in the conference, held by the Presbyterian Women's Fellowship. The workshop, for women leaders, drew thirty-five women from various districts across Africa for awareness raising and action planning on how to raise the consciousness of other groups.

Describing Stamp as hardworking, perceptive, and with a good sense of humour and the ability to laugh at herself, Ofei-Aboagye says Stamp's sensitivity is crucial to her success. "She is quick to pick up nuances, and that's what makes her work so rich.

"What really gets her fired up is when she thinks someone is being cheated, in the sense of their rights being trampled. She is excited by any sign of affirmative action. Anything that indicates an effort to improve one's situation meets with her support. That's why she was interested in our workshop, because many think the church has not been very helpful in advocating women's rights. So the idea that the women of the church could use it as an agent of change really excited her."

Asked if an abhorrence of injustice is what motivates her so strongly, Stamp replies: "Looking at that another way, I get very excited by flowerings of the human spirit and human community, wherever one finds them, whether it be a Maasai manyatta or a York classroom."

Her sense of duty also keeps her working to collect information and spread the word. Stamp says she is coming to terms with her feeling that she has to take on the role as elder. "Here's the grey hair, and I feel it my duty to act my age, status, and knowledge at this point. I feel it is my responsibility to assert my authority as an expert, well-grounded in the feedback I get from people like Esther and other colleagues and allies, who believe in a sisterly alliance — not that we believe that we are all sisters under the skin, but because these particular women and I believe in collaboration, that the future of the world, not just women, is going to lie in these kinds of generous cross-cultural collaborations," she says earnestly. With a smile, she then thrusts her fist into the air with a rallying cry: "Truth, justice, women, society, villages!"

Kirsteen MacLeod is a Toronto-based writer whose articles have appeared in Maclean's, The Financial Post, The Toronto Star, The Globe and Mail, *and* Toronto Life.

About the Institution

The International Development Research Centre (IDRC) is committed to building a sustainable and equitable world. IDRC funds developing-world researchers, thus enabling the people of the South to find their own solutions to their own problems. IDRC also maintains information networks and forges linkages that allow Canadians and their developing-world partners to benefit equally from a global sharing of knowledge. Through its actions, IDRC is helping others to help themselves.

About the Publisher

IDRC BOOKS publishes research results and scholarly studies on global and regional issues related to sustainable and equitable development. As a specialist in development literature, IDRC BOOKS contributes to the body of knowledge on these issues to further the cause of global understanding and equity. IDRC publications are sold through its head office in Ottawa, Canada, as well as by IDRC's agents and distributors around the world.